Mass Media and Development

MASS MEDIA AND DEVELOPMENT

Naval Prabhakar
Narendra Basu

Commonwealth

Mass Media and Development

Edition : 2019

ISBN 81-311-0021-9

Published by :
COMMONWEALTH PUBLISHERS PVT. LTD.
e-mail : commonwealthbooks@gmail.com

Distributed by :
CAMPUS BOOKS INTERNATIONAL
ARPAN PUBLICATIONS
4831/24, Prahlad Street,
Ansari Road, Darya Ganj,
New Delhi - 110002
Ph. : 23275511, 23257835
e-mail : arpanpublications@gmail.com
campusbooks@hotmail.com

Typesetting by :
Rishu Computers
Delhi

Printed at :
Divine Digital Press
Delhi

Preface

Knowledge and information are essential for people to respond successfully to the opportunities and challenges of social, economic and technological changes, including those that help to improve agricultural productivity, food security and rural livelihoods. The mass media are the primary channel of communication in our society. They provide information and education, personal identity, entertainment and most importantly integration and social interaction by giving insight into the circumstances of others as well as by helping with the development of social empathy.

Communication for development encompasses many different media and approaches — folk media and traditional social groupings, rural radio for community development, video and multimedia modules for farmer training, and the Internet for linking researchers, educators, extensionists and producer groups to each other and to global information sources.

As the mass media play a key role in community development it is incumbent upon the ethnic press to keep the communities connected to the past by communicating the stories and traditions we hold dear and to connect the communities to the present and to the future by delivering images and news of the people around the world and forming the foundation and values for our children to continue. Instead of undermining each other, the print and broadcasting media abroad should give the communities a strong voice that is not always represented in the mainstream media in the developed countries.

The present volume analyses the role of mass media in the development of communities. In various chapters, it focuses the application of development communication in particular areas, such as agriculture, health, education, environment, population etc.

Naval Prabhakar
Narendra Basu

Contents

1

Communication for Development

Knowledge and information are essential for people to successfully respond to the opportunities and challenges of social, economic and technological changes. But to be useful, knowledge and information must be effectively communicated to people. More than 850 million people in developing countries are excluded from a wide range of information and knowledge, with the rural poor in particular remaining isolated from both traditional media and new information and communication technologies which would improve their livelihoods. Development programmes can only realise their full potential if knowledge and technology are shared effectively, and if populations are motivated and committed to achieve success.

Unless people themselves are the driving force of their own development, no amount of investment or provision of technology and inputs will bring about any lasting improvements in their living standards. Communication is central to this task in many ways. For example, it enables planners, when identifying and formulating development programmes, to consult with people in order to take into account their needs, attitudes and traditional knowledge. Only with communication will the project beneficiaries become the principal actors to make development programmes successful.Helping people at all levels to communicate empowers them to recognise important issues and find common grounds for action, and builds a sense of identity and participation in order to implement their decisions. On top of that, development involves change, new ways of doing things. Communication media and techniques can be powerful tools to advise people about new ideas and methods, to encourage adoption of those ideas and methods, and to improve training overall. Communication approaches are also invaluable for improved coordination and teamwork to manage development programmes, and to gain institutional support.

The Role of Communication

A decisive role can be played by communication in promoting human development in today's new climate of social change. As the world moves towards greater democracy, decentralization and the market economy, conditions are becoming more favourable for people to start steering their own course of change. But it is vital to stimulate their awareness, participation and capabilities. Communication skills and technology are central to this task, but at present are often underutilized. Policies are needed that encourage effective planning and implementation of communication programmes. Major changes and new emphases have appeared on the development scene. Societies are opening to debate and markets to individual initiative; privatisation and entrepreneurship are being encouraged; new technologies are becoming widely available; management of government services is gradually being relocated closer to the users, if not handed over directly to users themselves, in order to cut costs and seek partners more committed to effective implementation.

Indeed, a host of structural adjustments are profoundly affecting most aspects of production and human interaction. These structural adjustments make demands, and have direct economic and social effects on people. Governments of developing countries can no longer fulfil all social and regulatory services by themselves, especially in rural areas. Many economies are overwhelmed by the cost of servicing their foreign debt, and governments are under stringent requirement from international financial institutions to reduce spending. In their quest for greater cost-effectiveness in all their operations, governments must have the active support of, and a greater contribution from, the people.

Governments are thus obliged to seek new and perhaps unfamiliar partners, ranging from local leaders to people in a variety of non-governmental organisations. These people are accordingly obliged to shoulder new and perhaps unfamiliar responsibilities. Furthermore, as we near the end of the century, a number of specific issues have come clearly into focus as being central to socio-economic progress, equity, social stability, to the future of humanity- and perhaps even to its survival. The environment and its relation to sustainable agricultural development and food production present an enormous challenge.

A prime consideration is the proper use and conservation of natural resources. These resources are often degraded at the hands of impoverished rural people who have no immediate alternative for meeting their needs for land on which to grow food, and for fuelwood. Their abuse of forest areas, with the negative consequences of soil erosion and dwindling water resources, will only be halted through new schemes of employment and income generation and through applying conservation techniques. Such solutions, however, will have to be made acceptable to local people, many of whom will need considerable encouragement and training in new skills. The provisions of Agenda 21, which emerged from the UN Conference on the Environment and Development held in Rio de Janeiro (1992), will only become a reality through large-scale changes in attitudes and behaviour in societies worldwide. Population growth is exerting pressure on natural resources, on food production and on the ability of governments to provide basic services and employment opportunities. Population growth depends on choices made by individuals. Helping people to make more informed choices by raising their awareness of the implications of family size and unwanted pregnancy, and of methods of contraception, requires much more than simply sending out messages. Instead it requires learning, from people and their leaders, how to make such issues socially acceptable and worthy of urgent action. Insight into people's underlying attitudes are needed before they can be helped to change their views.

Rural poverty continues to increase in many countries, accelerating urban migration and creating intolerable economic and social problems. The solution, of course, lies in the development of rural areas. Most rural communities are characterised by reliance on traditional knowledge and production systems, based strictly on what has worked for survival in the past. This has led to a view that rural communities are resistant to change, even though their traditional wisdom has been hard-won and its reasoning is sound. Planners need to take this into account, as the first step of any planning exercise.

For this, and for all rural development activities, communication between local communities and national planners and policy-makers is of vital importance but, unfortunately, in rural areas it is at its weakest. Malnutrition is both a cause and a consequence of underdevelopment. Recent decades have seen consistent reductions in the daily per caput supply of calories in many countries. The International Conference on Nutrition held in December 1992 drew attention to the fact that more than 780 million people in the world suffer from chronic malnutrition and that, each year, some 13 million children below the age of five die from infectious diseases that can be directly or indirectly attributed to hunger or malnutrition.

Nutritional well-being is not just a question of food availability and economics among families, however. It also depends on sufficient knowledge and acceptance of appropriate diets. At the planner's level, incorporating nutritional concerns into development initiatives for agriculture, food security, forestry, land use, exports and so forth requires an increased awareness of nutritional priorities since these are not spontaneously identified in such disciplines.Women in development is another priority issue. In many countries, women shoulder most of the work in rural areas.

Given the opportunity, women have shown themselves again and again to be highly responsive and responsible when helped to mobilise themselves, build upon available resources and produce sustainable results. Women need to learn additional technical and organisational skills and more women are needed at the centre of decision-making. Specific challenges where communication is vital include helping women's groups to increase their self-determination and to broaden the dialogue between the sexes regarding rights, privileges and responsibilities.

People and Communication

The first common theme running through the development issues just outlined is the human factor: the outcome will be based less on scientific and material inputs than on the people involved. For, even if our understanding of the development process is changing, there can be no doubt that its future shape, its pace, sustainability and ultimate direction - for better or worse - will be determined by people, and the level of their awareness, participation and skills. Investment in scientific and material inputs will bear no fruit without a parallel investment in "human capital" - in informing people, opening up avenues by which they may reach consensus for action, and developing the knowledge and skills needed to put material investments to the best use. Communication is the second common theme in the issues outlined. For if development can be seen as a fabric woven out of the activities of millions of people, communication represents the essential thread that binds them together. On the one hand, communication as dialogue and debate occurs spontaneously in any time of social change. The increased freedom of expression in recent times has been almost simultaneous with changes in the global political structure. On the other hand, it is communication as a deliberate intervention to affect social and economic change that holds the most interesting possibilities.

A development strategy that uses communication approaches can reveal people's underlying attitudes and traditional wisdom, help people to adapt their views and to acquire new knowledge and skills, and spread new social messages to large audiences.

The planned use of communication techniques, activities and media gives people powerful tools both to experience change and actually to guide it. An intensified exchange of ideas among all sectors of society can lead to the greater involvement of people in a common cause. This is a fundamental requirement for appropriate and sustainable development.

The rural dilemma

Nearly 1 000 million people in developing countries, more than one-third of the adult population, are illiterate. Rural communities are often remote and difficult to reach; they lack the infrastructures and communication systems - such as newspapers, radios, televisions and telephones, as well as meeting rooms, offices and schools -that help townsfolk keep abreast of developments and function effectively as informed participants. In rural areas, the challenge is to increase the quantity and accessibility of information, to ensure its exchange in appropriate ways, and to elicit more information from rural people themselves in order to guide development planning.

Technological advances

We live in a communication era, with rapid expansion in the reach of mass media, and improved techniques for the interpersonal exchange of ideas. The advent of the cheap transistor radio, for example, has brought this medium to remote corners of even the least-developed countries, where a lack of electricity can be overcome by solar-powered transmitters and receivers.Video provides a good example of the technological advances in the communication field. Little more than a decade ago, video was a bulky and expensive medium.

Preparation of printed materials with type, graphics and photographs, has also been revolutionised. The use of computers for desktop publishing has sharply reduced costs and production time, providing much greater access and versatility. Traditional and popular media such as folk theatre, dances, puppet shows and popular poetry, as well as rural press linked to literacy programmes, and audiovisual materials, can be highly effective channels for disseminating development information and for stimulating community action. Much more is now known about the interpersonal communication skills development field workers need in order to function more effectively as agents of change with rural people. These skills include the use of techniques such as focus group discussions, illustrated discussion tools such as flipcharts that have been pretested to be effective for rural viewers, and other media such as video and audiovisuals that can be used to share ideas and cause reflection, or as part of a training methodology involving presentation, discussion and practice. Interpersonal communication skills can improve activities at all levels, enhancing management, teamwork and the morale of personnel.

Communication for Better Planning

Any development programme that regards people as mere recipients, rather than as the actual creators of change and progress, usually fails. Consulting the people and actively involving them in making the decisions that will affect them virtually ensures the programme's success. In practical terms, effective planning must make a deliberate effort to determine what people want to do, can do and can continue to do in a sustainable way. To find this out, communication techniques go far beyond the simple question-and-answer survey. Meaningful discussion, generated by people trained in interpersonal communication skills, and audiovisual tools, such as video or radio, can help the community to identify its true problems and priorities and where its capabilities and needs lie.

This self-analysis can help a community to generate realistic proposals for new development initiatives and stimulates tremendous interest to have these initiatives succeed. The views of rural people can also guide prospective work plans, preventing them from moving in the wrong direction.

For example, agricultural research can be tied directly to what farmers really want and are capable of using. A systematic communication process brings researchers and practitioners together. A policy of communicating with people intensively before a development programme is even drafted, and taking into account their views, capabilities and needs as they see them, is the best insurance a planner can have.

People's Participation and Community Mobilisation

The dynamic strategy behind people's participation and community mobilisation is to release the energy of rural people by building their confidence to make decisions and carry them out as a community in a self-reliant way. and to grove that A. they benefit from such efforts. Communication activities can help people, even those from different social groups within a community, to share information and exchange ideas in a positive and productive fashion.

This dialogue can be enriched by understanding how development issues affect them, discovering what others think in other communities, and seeing what other communities have achieved. These are effective methods to help people to reach a consensus and find common grounds for action, based on their own needs and capabilities. Dialogue can be initiated and guided by field staff who have good interpersonal communication skills. Discussion tools such as flipcharts, audio-cassettes, slides and even video, can be used to help people visualize and reflect upon their own reality. Rural radio too can be a popular forum where local people do most of the talking about technical and cultural topics. These activities can lead to a serious diagnosis of problems and a search for solutions. Gaining people's participation always requires much face-to-face work within the community in order to make a bridge of understanding. Communication skills and media help people to visualize and cross that bridge more swiftly.

Changing life-styles

Rural populations, and women in particular, find it increasingly difficult to cope with rapidly changing social conditions, which often lead to the development of unsettling life-styles. For instance, in societies where marriage and childbearing no longer go together, the social and economic cost of teenage pregnancies weighs heavily on people's, and the nation's, resources. In others, rural youth, often from fatherless homes, increasingly rebels against parental poverty. Pressed by peers, teenagers often drop out of school, fall for drugs, or end up in the gangs of city slums. Communication can focus on the long and sensitive process of changing behaviour and life-styles. Quite recent communication research methodologies make it possible to gain insight into the underlying reasons why people adopt a certain life-style. Once this understanding is acquired, communication approaches can respond in a combination of ways. Mass media can raise awareness and public understanding of the social implications of problems such as adolescent fertility, AIDS or drug abuse. Other communication activities can bring about informed processes of change among the audiences they intend to reach. Interpersonal communication techniques such as peer counselling have the capacity to develop coping mechanisms, self-esteem and images of a better future among teenagers, especially if combined with group discussions and other tools which create a dialogue. Social communication activities based, for example, on street and village theatre, and using truly participatory methodologies, can pioneer attitudinal changes at the community level and stimulate nonthreatening environments in which teenagers wish to learn about life.

Communication for Improved Training

Colourful, even dramatic, audiovisual tools bring alive new ideas and techniques; they energise programmes of training and human resource development whenever they are used. Audiovisual materials can be produced locally at a reasonable cost. Then, duplicated in quantity, they can help to train large numbers of people. Audiovisuals have many additional advantages for users. Trainees - even if they are illiterate - can see and discuss quite complex techniques and procedures before practising them. This audiovisual training method improves mental retention enormously: making it four or five times better than just hearing a lecture, and nine times better than merely reading the information. In just one sitting a training group using audiovisuals can explore, for example, improved agricultural practices from sowing to reaping, the problem of deforestation and the solution of afforestation, or the symptoms of undernutrition and how people can obtain a better diet. Trainees can travel - through pictures - to places that are otherwise too distant and expensive to visit. Limits of time and space can be overcome, thanks to the skillful use of communication media. The trainers and field staff themselves also benefit from using audiovisual training packages. The technical information presented is standardised and of high quality, coming directly from technical specialists without any intervening distortion; the presentations are attractive and interesting; and the training packages guide dialogue from beginning to end. Overall audiovisuals allow trainers to be more confident and professional. The priority need for better training in agriculture and rural development can be illustrated by the tragic example of the use of agrochemicals.

Rapid spread of information

Often the news, as well as information on new techniques and issues of development should be made known to people throughout a region or an entire country. Used with skill, the mass media can provide a powerful service to spread this information far and wide. The use of radio, television, other electronic media and newspapers has grown considerably in many developing countries over the last four decades. The cost of using these media to spread information to large numbers of people can be low.

For example, studies have shown that radio broadcasts are 2 000 to 3 500 times less expensive per contact hour than extension workers are. Of course, extension workers do much more than pass messages, but the cost-efficiency of the mass media can be indisputable for certain purposes. One example comes from Turkey where free-of-charge "public-service" television time was given ; to air spots and programmes on health and social ~ themes such as teenage pregnancy.

Universally, whether media organisations are state-owned or in private hands, they and their audiences want interesting material. This is where good communication skills are essential to identify, to write and produce informational materials in a professional way. Building such skills among national staff for these purposes should be a priority.

Effective Management and Coordination

When a new development orientation is being introduced within a ministry, when strengthened teamwork is needed, or when planners and policymakers need to keep abreast of the field situation regarding the social effect of their development programmes, communication approaches are crucial. Workshops that bring together different levels of officials can be the best way to create common understanding and to obtain acceptance for change and a commitment to work together.

Such workshops, if well run, can be a rewarding exercise in communication skills. Participants from various levels can explore problems and opportunities in their development work and look for solutions, in a brain-storming atmosphere. Informal discussions allow centrally based managers to hear about the field situation in ways that are perhaps more meaningful than official reporting often is. They can also enter into the spirit of teamwork by helping to suggest new approaches and learning to work in a participatory way among staff of all levels. This experience boosts morale and commitment and provides insights into how participatory planning can work in practice. Media materials, such as rural radio and video programmes, which feature rural people themselves as a prime source of information, can have an additional purpose beyond their use in rural areas. They can provide management with direct raw information and a barometer of people's concerns, which otherwise might not pass so quickly through an administrative reporting process. Field staff, too, greatly appreciate the higher quality of information which communication techniques can provide as a supplement to the existing system of reports, memoranda and directives.

Regular, accessible and credible communications can narrow the gap between headquarters and the field. Used for reporting purposes, video, photographs, sound recordings and printed materials can bring the field situation alive to managers who may not have the means or the time to visit project sites.

Generating the Support of Decision-makers

Decision-makers in government, technical agencies and donor countries should be well informed about the progress and achievements of new programmes in order to sustain, and even expand them when justified. Communication tools can be a dynamic means to gain the attention and support of decisionmakers.

For presentations in meetings and displays at conferences, the use of video programmes, photographs, audiovisual programmes and overhead projections helps participants to visualize the otherwise dry statistics and data typed in reports. Video programmes are especially useful because they can be given to decision-makers to view individually at a convenient time, away from the pressures and distractions of office hours. Interesting programmes aired on national television and radio, and informative articles newspapers are often noticed by decisionmakers. Newsletters too, while primarily intended for people within development programmes, also keep decision-makers informed about achievements and needs. Deforestation is often a complex problem requiring complex solutions. If governments are to make informed decisions in-depth explanations from technical specialists and the serious attention of national policy-makers are needed. Unfortunately many policy-makers simply do not have the time.

Farmers around the world cite the advantages of setting ablaze agricultural land before planting crops: weeds are cleared, potent nutrients of ash are deposited on to the soil, and rodents, insects and other pests are destroyed. Tradition is not always best, however. The soil, in many places, is overworked and degraded - literally blowing away. Fires, occasionally out of control, devastate forest reserves and the desert advances.

The morale of forestry officers is greatly improved. Said one officer who received the communication training: "Before, people saw us as the agents of repression. This training taught us that from now on we shall be the agents of development in villages, alongside the population!" Rural radio programmes can be important tools for a variety of purposes such as promoting an antibushfire campaign .

Whether produced at the local, regional or national level, such radio programmes are most effective when made with audience participation, in local languages and taking into account cultural traditions. To achieve this, radio production teams should be multidisciplinary and mobile so that they can dialogue with many people and record a wide variety of important subjects for transmission.In this way, rural radio programming, besides spreading information, can fulfil other important functions: it can stimulate a regular discussion and debate among the people involved in development; provide a forum where rural communities can express their views and their cultural heritage; and it can even be a powerful means of investigation for decision-makers, helping them to appreciate better rural people and their world, in order to approach them in appropriate ways.

Developmental Programmes

Communication succeeds when it is part of the core strategy to set development priorities and carry out planning, implementation and evaluation of programmes, and also when it is used to improve training at all levels.There must be research, clear objectives, identification of different audience groups, careful message design and choice of channels, and monitoring and feedback. Multimedia approaches that use different communication channels in a coordinated and mutually reinforcing way give the best results. The last-minute addition of a "communication component" too often consists only of a budget to make project publicity materials or to produce some audiovisual aids, and is not cost-effective. A critical mass of staff, equipment and activities is needed to make an impact. Since the activities involve what is sometimes termed "social engineering", they must be persistent over time.

Media hardware may need to be purchased after determining clear objectives, needs and local infrastructure. An adequate maintenance facility is needed locally, and equipment operators must be trained in its use.The overall budget for communication, experience shows, is typically about 10 percent of the total development programme budget. For large-scale programmes, however, it may be as low as 1 percent, and for small programmes somewhat higher than 10 percent.Communication for development is a specialized field, and if local expertise is not available, technical assistance will need to be sought from neighbouring countries, from international agencies and aid programmes.

Communication Development Policy

A political and executive decision that development must reflect the true needs of people, and involve them every step of the way - this is the starting-point. Once this decision has been made at the highest level, and once it has been recognised that communication must be used to invigorate and sustain the development process, several policy issues of a more practical nature must be addressed in order to mandate a sphere of action for communication, to locate an institutional framework and ensure its operational requirements are met. A national communication policy should he drawn up to articulate the role of communication in development. This policy might require, for example, that communication and a participatory planning process should help to establish needs and guidelines prior to formulating any new development proposals, especially those involving rural communities. Alternatively, a somewhat less ambitious policy might simply ensure that communication activities and the media are used systematically to guide and promote the objectives of development programmes which are already established. Whatever the emphasis, communication for development should be conceived as a cross-cutting sector, similar to the already existing sectors of information, education and planning. It should cover subject matter where people's participation is needed, such as agriculture, livestock, forestry, environment, fisheries, population, women, health arid nutrition. The existing situation in most countries where sectoral ministries conduct their communication and extension work independently is proving wasteful, and the lack of coordination causes confusion. New legislation may be needed. For example, establishing a rural radio service that includes community radio stations where local people create and broadcast their own programmes could require new regulations or laws. In some countries the broadcasting channels, although belonging to the state, now expect ministries to pay for any services they require, and thus new financial relationships may need to be established within the government. To generate new sources of funding for communication and training activities, paid corporate sponsorship might be considered. An institutional framework should provide the logistical and organisational structure for communication work. In the past, large development programmes have sometimes had their own communication units consisting of planners, researchers, trainers and media producers, and a multimedia production capacity. In other cases, a central unit belonging to the technical ministry concerned has been used, as has the media infrastructure of the ministry of information.

A development communication policy and programming unit might be located in the decision-making centre of government. Here, it could keep abreast of the most recent national policies and objectives, advise decision-makers about communication issues and set the overall priorities for communication work. Within those overall priorities, the unit's main role could be to guide and support ministries, other development institutions, people's organisations, and other participants in the development process, in the planning, implementation and evaluation of their communication work. The unit could ensure a coordinated approach among all the partners in the development effort, and avoid having contradictory messages sent to the public. It could continuously analyse results, feedback, problems and opportunities revealed by the communication process, and inform the nation's policy-makers. Staffing of the unit would need to be small in number but high in professional quality, and a policy framework to give the unit the prestige necessary for it to carry out its planning and coordinating functions would be required.

The services for research, planning and media production and use could be arranged in a number of ways, depending on the circumstances. In many countries, individual ministries already have units for producing programmes for mass media and audiovisual training materials. In some cases, these may wish to continue independently, but with support, advice, training and coordination arranged by the central communication unit. In other cases, existing units may wish to amalgamate and perhaps form a parastatal service; and in others, ministries may decide to contract out their media research and production requirements to NGOs or the private sector, as is already happening in the field of health. Small countries may decide to establish a single communication service to handle all development needs. In some cases, NGOs might be entrusted with the whole task. There are a number of options, but whichever one is chosen, an important principle is that the communication services should aim to become financially autonomous, at least in part, within a given time-frame. This could be a precondition for their establishment. However, profit considerations should not be allowed to detract from the essentially public and social nature of the services provided. To generate income, the service or services would need a marketing plan to sell skills and capacities in areas such as field research, situation analysis, formulating communication strategies, producing media materials and training personnel in communication skills. Clients would be government ministries, institutions, aid agencies, NGOs and even commercial firms.

The goal of financial autonomy should directly guide the design of the services and their institutional framework. In many countries, parastatal structure might be the solution. This can allow income to be generated, retained and used directly by the communication service for its operational needs, rather than having income revert to the central treasury, as is usually the case when government departments earn revenue. The parastatal structure would also allow the service to pay higher salaries to trained communication personnel to avoid the risk of losing them to the private sector and to encourage greater creativity and problem-solving capability by the management. The establishment of such a parastatal institution usually needs legislative action. Training national personnel in communication for development would be vital in most cases.

Good communication staff possess a unique mix of knowledge and skills in social sciences as well as in the production and use of media. This particular educational curriculum still needs to be established in most countries. Common practice is to take social scientists or people with field experience in rural communities and train them in the use of communication media and the concept of rural development. Less frequently, media specialists are trained to use their skills to meet the needs of rural people. Managers may also need training in how to select outside contractors, such as advertising agencies with a social focus, and how to supervise them properly. Training of national staff in development communication is often best done in-country, based on the specific needs and with the media facilities and equipment available. However, the need to introduce very specialized media production techniques or provide higher level academic training may sometimes warrant external study.A mandate within the national communication policy and legislation may be needed for those who carry out communication activities so that they are recognised by others, and their scope of activities is well defined and directed. A clear mandate to use communication techniques, skills and media specifically to involve people in planning, participation and training for sustainable development, for example, would be useful. This would help to clear up any possible confusion between "communication for development" and public information, journalism or even some sort of political exercise.

Training the network of field staff, including extension staff, in the ministries might be another requirement, since the use of communication media with rural communities should be complemented by good interpersonal communication. Field staff should also learn how to gather feedback from rural communities in order to inform the managers of development programmes. Such liaison work gives field staff a new role and responsibility, and can deepen their commitment to achieving sustainable results.

CHALLENGE FOR PLANNERS

To take advantage of communication for sustainable development a progressive series of steps needs to be taken. As these steps are taken, a fundamental caution must be kept in mind. Are governments, or local authorities, entering into communication processes with rural people as a genuine expression of a common cause? Likewise there are implications for international development agencies.

And since meaningful social change takes time, can development programmes be planned accordingly, in terms of duration, budgets and criteria for evaluation? Applying communication to development emphasises the human element and, especially in a climate of social change, communication can support development in ways that are both known and new. To exploit its full potential is an enormous challenge. "Our common future" depends on meeting that challenge successfully.

A Look into the Future

With such rapid advances in communication technology and know-how, the age of telecommunication for rural development may already be upon us. Solar-powered microwave links for telephone communication, facsimile machines and even satellite links, are increasingly reaching into rural areas of the world, offering the possibility of breaking their traditional isolation for the first time in history.

In fact today the idea is being mooted that telecommunication learning centres could be established in villages of the developing world, with user-friendly computer terminals that would download interactive learning and management information programmes from a central supply, similar to a water or electricity service, with users paying modest charges for the time of actual use. The programmes could be video images, sound and computer-type data.

This technology already exists, and the speed with which it is becoming cheaper and more accessible is so rapid that the use of computers in the villages of developing countries may someday be part of a pragmatic strategy to reduce the rural-urban population shift and promote rural development. Whether we come to see village learning centres equipped with a centrally linked computer terminal, or, instead, a more systematic use of traditional media for human development, the use of communication no longer depends on the availability of technology: it depends on the will and decisions of policymakers to exploit its potential. Already communication has been highly exploited for political and commercial aims. Now is the time for communication to be applied to development.

2

Communication for Rural Development

For many years, people working to enhance telecommunication infrastructure and applications have referred to rural communities as being at the "last mile of connectivity." The concept of the "last mile" carries a lot of negative connotations and compels us to assume the perspective of an urbanite looking down at the rural margins. Titus Moetsabi was the first to turn this statement on its head and help us think instead of rural communities as being at the "first mile of connectivity." This term expresses a more equitable and far less urban-centric view of the challenge of providing everyone with the option of connecting themselves to the rest of the world and all it has to offer.

If rural communities are the "first mile," then the real challenge for enhancing rural connectivity lies with the urban-centred governments, businesses and agencies that have for so long ignored or placated the desires of rural people to get connected to the world. The challenge is not technical or financial, but political and ideological. From the vantage point of a rural community in a developing country, getting connected with phone lines, payphones, community telecentres and even Internet services is not a luxury or an "inappropriate" use of technology for development.

For a rural person, getting connected is a means for sharing the wide range of options available to urbanites, a means for making better and more informed decisions, a means for staying in contact with friends and families who migrate to urban areas for work and education, a means for linking their businesses to the trade, transportation and commerce systems of urban areas, and a means for accessing the services (health, education, information, etc.) that enable urban people to improve their lives.

Many urban people, and many of those who make decisions about allocation of development resources, take the privilege of connectivity for granted. Until one has experienced the daily difficulties and knowledge access deficits faced by the "great un-wired" of the world, then one has no business deciding what is, or should be, in their best interests. Those of us who advocate for improved rural telecommunication infrastructure and applications in developing countries are used to hearing urban decision-makers question the drive for rural connectivity. Rural people in developing countries are quite adept at appropriating Western technologies for their own goals and objectives. Rural people have every right to desire and demand the tools that help improve quality of life, health, prosperity and cultural vibrancy.

Despite the positive thrust of the "first mile" perspective, there are some dangers in pushing for rural connectivity at any cost. It is possible for any technology to be used inappropriately if the technology is beyond the control and influence of those who would use it. Solutions for rural connectivity are best developed with and for rural people. Rural people must be enabled to participate in making decisions about how and where telecommunication technologies will be put to use. Access to the technologies, and influence on their use, must be equitable across the diverse groupings within rural communities. To be sustainable, rural telecommunication technologies need to be designed with rural people as active participants in strategizing, planning, implementing and evaluating.

The field of "communication for development" has a long legacy of the critical application of technologies, particularly communication technologies, for development. This book is designed to bring together the practitioners, perspectives and lessons-learned from that field to add new understandings and knowledge for the advancement of telecommunication technologies for rural development.

Whether we like it or not, these new technologies are rapidly finding their way into some rural communities while other rural communities are being left off the connectivity map indefinitely. For some unknown reason, few communication for development practitioners have ever considered tools such as telephones to be of significant value in the technological toolkit of communication for development practice. We have worked for decades with rural community radio, participatory video and print applications, but we have tended to ignore telephones, fax machines and newer telecommunication applications such as the Internet. At the same time, rural telecommunication experts, technicians and engineers, may find that their rural systems are poorly used, poorly maintained and money losing because they have not followed the basic communication for development prescription of peoples' participation in technological choice and development.

Communication, the process whereby various participants are linked and can exchange information, is an essential element of sustainable development. Participatory communication, then, is an "enabling" process that allows for the development of relevant technology, the empowerment of local organizations, and the effectiveness of external institutions. In light of this, rural development professionals and telecommunication experts need to develop the capacity to facilitate healthy interaction among stakeholders. This will encourage local groups to become active promoters of development and ensure the sustainability of the process.

Viewing information and communication technologies (ICTs) as tools for development, he encourages community workers to develop appropriate skills to use these tools. He places a high priority on being involved with the targeted community and on allowing community members as much control over the process as possible. He believes that learning catalysed by effectively employed ICTs will be embraced by communities and lead to long-term development. If sustainable development is achieved through a participatory communication approach, then the initial stage of research should reflect the same ideals as the entire process. Research becomes an interactive process, allowing the community to learn about itself. This ensures that the transforming processes initiated will reflect the realities of the rural community, encouraging the sustainability of the development. The approach may yield many benefits if used during the initial stages in the development of ICT applications and telecommunication systems, with and for rural communities.

In Radio and video for development the ideals of participatory development, coupled with recent technological revolutions, are changing the way communication media are used, and who uses them. Fresh methods are overturning the traditional "top-down" approach to communication, are encouraging situation specificity, and are involving broadcasting professionals in the community in which they are serving. Although such participatory communication techniques have been used since the 1960s, it is only recently that practitioners have started sharing their experiences to arrive at a common understanding of the principles of participation and communication. The emerging participatory communication approach allows the poor to access communication technology to influence their social and political environment. This is a particularly relevant perspective with regard to advancing telecommunication for rural development. The use of radio documentaries to promote sustainable, democratic development provides a powerful example of participatory communication at work. The lessons gained from this successful learning experience can be applied to the use of various ICTs in promoting sustainable development. The analysis of the combination of rural radio documentaries and radio "phone-in" audience participation provides an important example of the marriage of media such as telephones and radio in development initiatives.

The rural and remote areas need advanced telecommunications and information technology to support their public services, business enterprises, and educational systems. Low-cost technology is available to set up effective rural networks, but lack of awareness of the technology and lack of skills in using it are formidable obstacles to its integration in communities. Community telecentres - centres that make available a range of information and communication technology facilities to people who cannot individually afford such services - can provide rural communities with access to advanced technology and efficient services that are comparable to the services available in urban centres. At the same time the staff of the telecentres can provide training to those unfamiliar with the technology, ensuring that the community members are able to use the services. Innovative methods of involving rural communities in the global village will require the appropriate use of telecommunication tools to overcome the barriers to participation.The poor telecommunication infrastructure of the African continent prevents its rural inhabitants from accessing the benefits of inexpensive, reliable services.

Telecommunications is recognized as a major force supporting economic and social development. The five key principles as a framework for providing rural and remote areas with telecommunication services. Provision of universal access, efficient rural programmes, an appropriate regulatory framework, internal and investment financial resources, and a commercial approach are principles that will lead to profitable and valued telecommunication systems. These systems need to be effectively maintained, expanded and enhanced to secure their continuing commercial viability and community support. Enhanced communication services and accessibility of information are related to social and economic development. In the "global village," the privileged are those with access to information; typically these people reside in urban areas. Rural people, particularly the food-insecure, must be given the opportunity to obtain relevant information, to communicate and to plan their own development efficiently.

The Internet is a flexible, decentralized, information-sharing tool and has the potential to support a variety of rural development endeavours. It offers the possibility of initiating economic development for agricultural producers, expanding the effectiveness of community development programmes, increasing the amount of participatory research conducted, promoting small business enterprises, and improving news media networks. If used as a tool for encouraging two-way communication processes and creating links between people, then it may open up new opportunities for rural people to participate in the global society.

A deeper orientation to the participatory communication for development methodologies through which Internet applications can enhance and promote food security. Involving community members in the analysis of problems and respecting their ownership of local decisions will result in development that meets the members' real felt needs. The Internet is a tool that may promote participatory communication, but only if its design and implementation are done in a participatory manner. Communities need to understand the structure of the electronic system and participate in the design of a customized communication programme tailored for their interests, needs, and local culture. Approaching electronic communication development in this way allows communities to be prepared for the significant changes that could result from the ensuing rapid information exchange.

Community telecentres allow populations in rural and remote areas to participate exchanging information. They offer a practical and community-oriented way to bring new information and communication technologies to the service of rural people.The rural community telecentres can empower communities in the information society. Although the food-insecure may not place high priority on the development of ICTs in their community, access to such technology could prove to be vital to their economic development. Bringing such people into the "information society" requires two things: policies that encourage the growth of the telecommunication and information sector, and the development of efficient, accessible infrastructure.

Community telecentres are effective tools for development when integrated with a larger community development programme that involves all stakeholders. Before telecentres are adopted into national level programmes, developers need to study the impact of the centres on rural and remote areas. Ernberg describes an International Telecommunication Union (ITU) programme aimed at establishing pilot projects in developing regions in order to further explore the issues related to the adoption of telecentres.

It is widely accepted that ICTs may support economic and social development, but a framework to guide the introduction of these technologies to developing regions is absent. A number of ideas that could be included in a set of guidelines for rural telecentres. In choosing the location of a telecentre, issues such as potential demand, its proximity to other institutions, and local infrastructure need to be addressed. A participatory assessment of local needs and skills, as well as an understanding of local communication processes and channels, should determine which services to develop. Community members need to be familiar with the services available to them, be encouraged to implement their own applications, and be involved in all levels of the project's development.

Only by sharing experiences will development facilitators be able to avoid the pitfalls of "top-down" technology transfer. It is hoped that professionals will reflect on their own experiences and add to these ideas to arrive at a common set of principles and guidelines for developing rural telecentres.

Participatory jargon is prevalent in communication for development discussions and theories, but using the fashionable terms does not guarantee that development activities reflect participatory ideals.Training community animators as participatory communication for development practitioners, and sheds some light on what might be involved in training future generations who will work more and more with rural telecommunication technologies. If we are to facilitate participatory communication among the communities with whom we work, we must make a conscious effort to practise it ourselves. It is not enough to ask community workers to work within the participatory framework; the training of these workers needs to be participatory. Such training programmes should focus less on technological skill and, using a flexible learner-directed approach, allow learners to develop the relational skills needed to facilitate participation. Giving learners the opportunity to learn by doing ensures that the experience is relevant to future work. Instructors, then, need to be facilitators, participants, and "relators" instead of merely being experts in communication technology.

The complex organizational dynamics that can challenge facilitators of rural telecommunication initiatives. He describes how creative alliances were forged to create a sustainable and useful network in rural areas. Facilitating such alliances is not easy, but dedicated rural telecommunication advocates, working with participatory approaches, can help organizations realize substantial cost savings and mutual benefits. One of the unique spin-offs of developing rural telecommunication systems is the way that such projects can catalyse and energize new and dynamic relationships among organizations that previously had little contact with one another.

If rural communication programmes are to stay relevant, they must be closely monitored and evaluated. The current evaluations ignore the impacts that ICTs may have on the rural stakeholder communities. In an attempt to focus on the grassroots level, he proposes an evaluation framework to examine the effects that local connectivity has on unconnected rural stakeholders. In light of the value of the participatory communication approach to development, the communication rather than the end result, should be the target of ICT evaluations. Measuring the effectiveness, efficiency, and impacts of the NGOs' use of the Internet is essential to improving rural networks and developing ICT technologies for the people needing them most - rural stakeholders.

Enabling policies have a key role in encouraging rural telecommunication applications for development. The telecommunication services are increasing worldwide, the beneficiaries of these services are primarily citizens of developed nations or urban residents. Access to telecommunications is severely restricted in developing countries, particularly in rural areas. If it is agreed that universal access to information is crucial for development, then developing nations should adopt the goal of providing service for rural people that is comparable to their urban counterparts. Strategies designed to meet this need to take into account the rapid development of cheap, efficient telecommunication technologies, and the changing policy environment that emphasizes private sector investment. National telecommunication policies must adapt to changing user needs, reflect public interest, and incorporate incentives with sanctions in order to make telecommunication services universally available. Only within a favourable policy environment will these services become accessible to the rural members of developing countries.

Public policies that simply make telecommunication technologies available to rural residents will not guarantee their integration into and use by the communities in which they are deployed. Rural telephone companies have a wealth of experience in promoting the diffusion of telecommunication services in rural areas. The "best practices" of these organizations with the intention of arriving at a framework for determining appropriate telecommunication policies that build upon the strengths existing in rural institutions and communities. Communication services that benefit rural communities depend less on efficient technology than on effective implementation strategies. Previously successful implementation strategies have been community-based, rural-specific, and carried out through the cooperation of rural telecommunication providers. Effective state policies will recognize that communication services link people and bind communities together, and will capitalize on the strengths of local rural telecom organizations working in cooperation with one another and with their communities.

The argument that rural telecom services should be developed because of their socio-economic benefits is a common one, but the financial benefits of rural and remote services are assumed to be limited at best. The socio-economic benefits, financial revenues, and commercial viability are closely linked. Telecommunications is a potentially viable sector in every country, but this potential can only be realized through bold policies designed to attract private investors. Such policies will have the objectives of making rural telecommunication a financially attractive investment, and of making the developed services fully available to their users. The demand for telecommunication services exists, and within an appropriate policy environment this sector can capitalize on that demand to achieve maximum commercial and socio-economic benefits. ICTs are unique tools capable of encouraging sustainable economic and social development in rural and remote areas. Like any tool, they must be used skilfully in order for their potential to be realized. When integrated into a programme that envisions community participation and information sharing, communication systems become enabling forces for development. Successful implementation of these systems will require communication and development professionals to exchange past experiences and ideas for future directions. As we learn from one another we can move towards a shared framework for advancing telecommunication to support development - towards meeting the challenges of the "first mile".

Rural Telecommunication Systems

Rural telecommunication systems are powerful communication and knowledge sharing tools. They can bring new information resources and open up new communication channels to facilitate dialogue and the flow of information between rural people and their organizations, institutions and governments. Rural telecommunication systems are a means through which people can access new options to help make their lives more secure, prosperous and meaningful. By providing a relatively open and uncontrolled means for interaction, dialogue and information sharing, simple rural telephone kiosks and pay phones offer intriguing opportunities for adding value to sustainable development efforts. For example, they can enable the bottom-up articulation and sharing of information on local needs and local knowledge through providing a new and cost-effective means of communication.

Rural telecommunication systems can range from very basic pay telephones on the walls of village stores, to digital wireless cellular telephones and sophisticated community Internet systems. Transmission of voice and data can use a variety of tools, including wooden telephone poles and copper telephone lines, analogue radio transmitters and receivers, low earth orbit satellite systems, digital point-to-point microwave transmitters, towers and receivers, wireless local loops, fibre optic cables, or even local infrared light transmission and reception devices.

In recent years, we have seen the rapid spread of rural "telecentres" in developing countries. Telecentres are a grassroots business phenomenon. They are generally small shops providing pay phone telephone service, together with fax, photocopying and sometimes Internet services. They tend to be operated by local entrepreneurs and provide very useful and appropriate service to rural communities. Whatever their form, rural telecommunication systems are best described by their uses which enable rural people and their organizations to communicate and share information:

— within communities and villages;

— horizontally to other communities and villages;

— vertically to friends, relatives, peers, and government and non-governmental organizations (NGOs) in urban and international contexts.

Unfortunately, in today's knowledge-based economies there are those who are "information haves" and those who are "information have-nots," and there is a large gap between them. Often rural telephone systems will provide telephone lines and equipment only to local elites, government offices and homes of the police and local officials. Unless we can make tools like rural telephones more widely available, especially to the rural poor, then the expanded use of rural telecommunication systems among the "information haves" will further enlarge the gap with the "information have-nots." The source of the appeal of rural telecommunication systems as tools for development "isn't technology or information, but people," and their ability to share knowledge with one another.

The processes of globalization and the transformation of industrial and agricultural economies into economies increasingly based on information and knowledge infrastructure require us to devote considerable energy to enabling the information have-nots to gain access to telecommunication infrastructure that enables knowledge sharing. Without this access, the information have-nots will be at the mercy of external forces, with little or no ability to understand, respond or direct the forces that affect their lives.

With regard to rural telecommunication systems, it is imperative to find ways to put these systems within reach of the rural poor in concert with efforts to enable them to establish communication linkages with intermediary peoples' organizations, NGOs and government agencies that serve the poor. It is also imperative to find ways to enhance telecommunication linkages between the rural poor and their urban family members and friends who are attempting to help families and communities to achieve prosperity and better lives. When a rural person wants to start a business, find money to repair a village well or gain assistance with medical expenses, it is often an urban family member or friend who is the first contact for support and capital. Access to a simple village pay phone can make a world of difference.

Rural telecommunication systems open up entirely new channels and options for people to stay in touch with friends, family and peers. They enable rural people to instantaneously, inexpensively, reliably and globally communicate. Primary development benefits include increased efficiency in the use of development resources, opportunities to reduce duplication of activities and promote collaboration, reduction of communication costs, reduction in transportation costs, and global access to information and human resources used for planning, consultation decision-making and action. The biggest drawbacks of rural telecommunication systems are dependency on largely urban-centred telecommunication infrastructure, dependency on urban-centred telecommunication regulations and legislation governing ownership and operation, and generally low levels of telecommunication service standards in countries with monopolistic, expensive, state-run telecommunication systems.

Despite the drawbacks of rural telecommunication systems, there has been a rapid increase in the spread of these systems in developing countries. The spread can be quite dramatic, especially as rural people in developing countries gain access to digital telecommunication services that are still far out of the reach of many rural people. However, none of the potential developmental benefits of rural telecommunication systems will be fully realized by the technology of rural telecommunication systems alone. Potential development benefits are realized only when people, including development planners, development beneficiaries, private sector telecommunication providers, technical experts and other stakeholders, work together to plan, implement, use and evaluate both technical infrastructure and the human, organizational and developmental applications of the technology.

Current evidence suggests that to achieve sustainability and success, rural telecommunication projects designed to achieve development goals must begin with the real needs of intended beneficiaries . Intended beneficiaries in planning, design and implementation tend to focus less on telecommunication infrastructure and gadgets, and more on basic communication and information applications that meet peoples' needs. This kind of planning approach also yields improvements in the management of telecommunication operations and is directly related to improvement in the revenue received from the rural and urban users of rural telecommunication systems.

International Telecommunication Union (ITU) reports indicate that if people working in economic and social sectors who have a stake in rural areas are partners in supporting rural telecommunication services, then there is a greater likelihood that those services will be profitable and sustainable. Engaging rural stakeholders with an interest in rural development in matching development objectives with rural telecommunication opportunities can enable stakeholders to develop specific information and communication applications that serve development objectives. These same telecommunication applications that serve development objectives will increase telecommunication traffic and revenue.

Rural stakeholders can also provide a means for insuring that telecommunication operators receive support, encouragement and incentives for managing rural telecentres effectively. Where telecentres are managed poorly, rural stakeholders who have been partners in supporting rural telecommunication initiatives will be well placed to report operational and maintenance problems to telecommunication operators and government authorities. Thus, rural stakeholders can become both supporters and informal monitors of system operations. Influential citizens and politicians who have a stake in rural development can provide significant support and informal management advice to help enable telecommunication operators to sustain high levels of rural telecentre service.

Rural telecommunication initiatives can facilitate stakeholder engagement by providing opportunities for dialogue, exchange of ideas and problem solving prior to the implementation of a telecommunication infrastructure project. An example of such an opportunity would be, a series of simple workshops to assist rural stakeholders in understanding the potential of rural telecentres to support social and economic development. In particular, officials from existing national and regional development projects would be invited to participate in workshops designed to identify specific telecommunication applications that can assist planners, decision-makers, projects officers and rural people in achieving their social development and rural economic development objectives. Ideally, rural telecommunication initiatives will establish an ongoing rural stakeholder advisory group that can assist telecommunication operators to upgrade and enhance rural telecommunication services.

Ultimately, rural stakeholder engagement helps achieve both development goals and profitability for telecommunication operators: a win-win situation. One component of stakeholder engagement is to enable telecommunication operators to better identify opportunities to target specific client groups with services and marketing initiatives that will increase telecommunication traffic between rural telecentres and national and international callers. International traffic reaching rural telephone centres can be increased by informing international callers of creative methods for enabling them to contact friends and family in rural areas. At the local level, telecentre operators, franchises and their clients can be provided with strategic marketing workshops to enable them to develop marketing plans and follow-through with marketing initiatives that serve the needs of rural clients. This, of course, helps to generate the revenue necessary to sustain and continuously upgrade local telecommunication services. Such workshops will also enable telecommunication operators to clarify procedures to ensure that rural telecentre operators are capable of managing local services effectively.

Rural telecommunication service operators are usually provided with rather dry technical training, but get little or no training on ways of facilitating and enhancing stakeholder participation. Simple participatory training sessions in collaboration with rural stakeholders can go a long way in sensitizing operators to the needs of their local client groups. This can not only improve service, but can also improve the revenue streams that will sustain the local operator and their equipment. Technical training itself can be improved through the knowledge gained through stakeholder input. Stakeholder participation in the development of technical and service training materials can add a client-centred focus to training programmes. Creative use of participatory video training tools, which include testimonials from rural users and leaders, and involve rural stakeholders in articulating their concerns about proper maintenance and client satisfaction, will help operators to recognize the vital community role they play. Training videos developed using participatory techniques can help generate linguistically and culturally appropriate training content.

Rural telecentre maintenance and operation training videos will be developed in the local Creole dialect. These videos will use "star" telecentre operators who have good stakeholder relationships, together with local musicians and other local talent to help ensure audience attention and understanding. Training workbooks will be developed with the assumption that rural telecentre operators have low literacy skills and will include local photographs, graphics, easy-to-understand graphical flow charts and icons. All of these visually oriented training tools will be pre-tested with operators and stakeholders to ensure cultural appropriateness, efficacy and relevance. These same visual aids can be used in developing operation and reporting tools for telecentre management.

While there is currently a great deal of international donor and government attention and funds focused on the use of rural telecommunication systems for development purposes, the jury is still out on the potential developmental impact of these services. Today, we really have very little available evidence to unequivocally support claims for rural telecommunication systems' developmental benefits. At best, we have many compelling anecdotal reports on specific cases of farmers, health workers, people's organizations, and non-governmental organizations gaining benefits from such services.

We also have far too many stories of donor agencies supporting telecommunication services, especially Internet services, that benefit only elite researchers and institutional officials in developing countries, with little, if any evidence indicating that these services are actually improving the delivery of development programmes or enhancing research that has direct impact on development objectives. The need for research and evaluation of rural telecommunication services for development initiatives is abundantly clear and donor organizations appear to be recognizing this in increasing numbers, but the call for critical research and evaluation must continue. Rural stakeholder input within research and evaluation efforts is of paramount importance.

Rural Telecommunication Services

To designed to help bridge the gap between practices of the communication for development practitioners and telecommunication experts who provide services to rural areas. Improvements in technology and reductions in costs have focused new attention on the provision of rural telecommunication services, particularly in developing countries. Until very recently, communication for development practitioners have seldom looked at rural telecommunication services as development tools. Likewise, telecommunication experts have only recently begun to look at the synergy between communication for development practices and the spread of rural telecommunication systems. Working together, these two groups of practitioners can better understand the potentials, limitations and challenges of telecommunication systems for rural development.

The most important benefit of rural telecommunication systems lies in their use as tools for interpersonal communication, which is the foundation of communication for development. The term "communication for development" is used to describe processes of two-way dialogue and expression that encourage sharing of feelings, desires, beliefs and experiences, together with problem analysis, exploration of solutions, and bottom-up communication that raises the awareness of decision-makers to those problems. The basic tenet of communication for development is that the communication process is more important than the production of media products or content. Communication for development practitioners, then, are people with skill and experience in facilitating social and organizational interventions, and using various media to catalyse two-way communication, dialogue and problem-solving .

All development efforts, whether focused on technology diffusion or not, draw our attention to issues of participation, capacity building, power and control. In planning, implementing, using and evaluating telecommunication applications we must bridge the technical with the social, political, cultural and economic dimensions of development. In over five decades of development practice, communication for development practitioners have come to understand that interventions of a social or organizational nature, designed to catalyse the participation of stakeholders are of key importance in achieving development goals. Rural telecommunication systems can add new mechanisms for enabling and enhancing such participation, and for achieving a variety of other communication, information sharing and problem-solving applications that can assist development efforts.

Communication for development practitioners, of course, do not normally possess the technical expertise required to establish rural telecommunication systems and are thus dependent on the knowledge and skills of telecommunication experts to help establish these new mechanisms for enabling and enhancing participation. Collaboration between telecommunication experts and development practitioners can do much more than establish new information and communication technologies (ICTs) for enabling and enhancing participation. When added to the technical knowledge of rural telecommunication experts, the knowledge and skills of communication for development practitioners - particularly in the areas of stakeholder participation, training and organizational capacity building - can help ensure that technologies are developed appropriately and can achieve sustainability and revenue generation. Sustainability and revenue generation tend to be key goals in the establishment of rural telecommunication systems; however, telecommunication experts may not always possess the knowledge and skill necessary to facilitate the participatory processes that can help achieve these goals. Partnerships between our fields of knowledge and expertise are necessary.

The use of rural telecommunication systems for development purposes is limited by a lack of concerted action, dialogue and planning among groups of rural development stakeholders. Stakeholders include rural users themselves, private sector telecommunication companies, telecommunication equipment manufacturers and vendors, telecommunication regulatory agencies, non-governmental organizations working in sectors such as health, education, business improvement, credit and agriculture, educational institutions, and government agencies involved in rural development efforts. Rural telecommunication systems, where they exist at all, are typically planned, designed and installed by technicians and engineers who rarely consult with rural stakeholders. As a result, systems are installed with little imagination, creativity or opportunity to envision how they might help achieve developmental objectives.

Like the irrigation systems and mechanized agricultural tools of the Green Revolution, telecommunication services are often "dumped" into rural areas. The results, in terms of efficiency of use, revenue generation for rural telecommunication operators, and benefits to rural stakeholders, can be minimal. Phones may work for a while, but may be poorly maintained or made inaccessible by local operators who have little incentive to provide good service. Rural people may want to use phones, but have no idea who to call to gain access to specific information because simple telephone directories for agriculture, health and education contacts are unavailable. Friends and relatives, as well as urban organizations needing to contact rural fieldworkers, may want to call rural people, but because rural telephone kiosk numbers are not clearly posted or available, no one will know what number to dial. The development of creative applications of rural telecommunication systems, such as agricultural marketing information services, or health care worker assistance services, may be ignored by technicians who see telephones as simple voice communication tools.

As with other methods and tools used to facilitate development, telecommunication services work best when development stakeholders participate fully in planning, implementation, use and evaluation of those services.

The following key elements can facilitate or retard stakeholder participation.

- leadership commitment to a vision of development that involves stakeholder participation;
- investment in human resource development that facilitates stakeholder participation;
- clarity of rules and policies that encourage, reward and are informed by stakeholder participation;
- adequacy of budgetary resources required to achieve stakeholder participation;
- the coherence of policy frameworks that define the goals to be achieved through coordinated action and stakeholder participation;

— clarity of organizational responsibilities for encouraging, and learning from, stakeholder participation;

— effectiveness of specific mechanisms for interaction among organizations and incentives for individuals to interact with colleagues in other organizations, and stakeholders in general;

— effectiveness of horizontal interaction among levels of government engaged in collaborative work.

The challenge we face with telecommunication systems is how to convert the ideal of full stakeholder participation into reality, and ensure that these key elements favour and facilitate stakeholder participation.

The processes of globalization and the influence of global market forces are affecting virtually everyone in the world. Access to telephone systems, fax machines and Internet services currently provide the world's "information haves" with the means to participate in, influence and counter global market forces and the processes of globalization. Meanwhile, the world's "information have-nots" continue to find only erratic and difficult means for such participation: in many regions, participation may be impossible. Rapid advances in telecommunication and computer technologies, together with lower costs for these tools and related services, are making it possible for ever more people to have access to telephones, faxes and Internet systems. Poor rural areas that have never seen telephones are beginning to have access to advanced digital and microwave telephone systems and pay phones that are low cost and efficient.

Any development project that might include rural telecommunication systems ought to begin with assessments of the real needs of participants and use methodologies that catalyse participation and stakeholder engagement. This will help ensure that *if* rural telecommunication systems possess communication and information sharing characteristics that are attractive and relevant to intended participants, then those participants will be enabled to define and direct the development of applications that serve their needs. Ideally, local rural telecommunication applications for development purposes will be managed and maintained directly by the participants involved in the development effort in question.

Despite these participatory prescriptions, and despite very similar methodological prescriptions in the reports of some telecommunication analysts, efforts to catalyse participation and stakeholder engagement in development projects involving rural telecommunication systems are not the norm. It is too easy for the use of rural telecommunication systems to be driven by the technology, rather than by those who would supposedly benefit from its applications. A variety of tools from the fields of communication for development, participatory action research, and rapid knowledge systems appraisal and action can be used to catalyse participation and stakeholder engagement. These tools are seldom, if ever, applied, perhaps because the technical advocates of rural telecommunication systems rarely cross paths with people who work in the field of communication for development.

Finding opportunities for collaboration between communication for development practitioners and rural telecommunication advocates is of critical importance. The facilitation of the design and implementation of rural telecommunication applications for development requires the involvement of people experienced in fields such as community development, rural development, extension, gender and development, and communication for development.

Rural Telecommunication Initiatives

The value of a stakeholder participation within rural telecommunication systems may be difficult to understand until a person has an opportunity to participate in such an initiative. Telecommunication organizations that do not already have strong community communication and outreach orientations, are prone to scepticism and dismissal of stakeholder participation because they may feel fear about greater contact with the public and public criticism. This attitude can spell disaster for telecommunication operators that are moving from monopoly service contexts to liberalized and competitive contexts where a client-centred focus makes the difference between profit and bankruptcy.

If a telecommunication organization is not already functioning with participatory management styles, and a client-centred perspective, there may be little value in introducing stakeholder participation as a communication tool that can optimize communication flow. In liberalized and competitive contexts, new and more nimble operators with client-centred orientations may quickly move in to take the place of old "top-down" and inefficient telecom bureaucracies, no matter how hard those bureaucracies might resist. This is an important factor for facilitators of stakeholder participation to understand. It is necessary for facilitators to spend time in the early days of an initiative in order to get a better understanding of the complex nature of community, organizational and stakeholder politics, as well as leadership personalities and political manoeuvring.

If resistance to stakeholder participation is too strong within a particular telecommunication organization, it may be necessary to generate this participation first among stakeholders who can then assist in drawing client-centred telecommunication operators and individual managers into the process.

The keenest participants in stakeholder engagement processes involving rural telecommunication systems are people and organizations that are pre-disposed to participatory communication and participatory management styles. The facilitators, based at a university, were prompting a vision of a community owned and managed network that would neither be owned nor controlled by the university, but by community organizations. After experiencing frustrations with the lack of leadership, commitment and understanding among telecommunication operators, county government, libraries and school board officials, the facilitators found themselves evaluating prospective partners based not on the extent of their profile in the community, but based on prospective partners' existing record for participatory communication, openness and information sharing within the community.

Very quickly they noticed that the people and organizations with the most interest and commitment were organizations that were already deeply involved in various aspects of local community development, or providing meaningful local services. Start working with community organization leaders who instantly see the benefits of rural telecommunication services. Work with organizational leaders who are pre-disposed to collaborative, open and participatory communication approaches to community development. Do not expend too much time and energy attempting to convince organizational leaders who are pre-disposed to "turf wars," "empire building," and who demonstrate little regard for public participation processes. Their participation will follow, in due time, as rural telecommunication services gain popularity.

Real, risk-taking community leadership and advocacy for rural telecommunication systems is not necessarily found within elected bodies, telecommunication operator management and local government bureaucracies where one might normally expect to start looking. We should expect rural telecommunication champions to come from unexpected sectors of local, national and operator leadership.

Provide many opportunities for women and young people to actively participate and volunteer their time and energy for practical and identifiable tasks that support rural telecommunication systems. Recognize and reward their efforts at every opportunity, and provide mechanisms to ensure that they can participate in key management or advisory roles.

Provide human resource development support for rural telecommunication project management in the areas of project planning, evaluation, monitoring, facilitation of stakeholder participation, and leadership skills. Continuously remind all involved that, at its core, a rural telecommunication service has the dual goals of sustaining itself through revenue generation and supporting rural development.

Rural telecommunication systems are unique and should be planned and implemented in unique ways, in consultation with rural stakeholders who best understand local contexts. Large, government initiated, top-down telecommunication systems that provide rural telecommunication services as an afterthought have a high failure rate, are generally unsustainable and can cost large amounts of money.

Build an energetic steering committee to assist in infrastructure deployment and stakeholder engagement. Rural telecommunication systems are ultimately about people, not technology. Build a team of enthusiastic proponents who come from diverse backgrounds. Do not stack a steering committee with "techies," or "urban elites." Actively seek people who know more about rural communities than telecommunication systems.

Always try to work with people who work with community-minded organizations or community development agencies. Their experience and contacts in the community will help ensure that you will find the resources and support you need. Good organizations with which to begin working include: service clubs, health clinics, churches, educational institutions involved with outreach and continuing education initiatives, libraries and non-governmental organizations involved in economic development. When linked together through improved communication systems, the power of such grassroots organizations can be multiplied by a hundred. At the same time they can use their telecommunication connections to enhance inter-agency collaboration, joint service offerings and joint planning.

Use local technical and human resource development expertise whenever possible, and provide necessary training and capacity building where the expertise does not currently exist. The ability to access local technical expertise and local training services will significantly enhance sustainability.

Take sustainability seriously rural telecommunication services must find creative ways to generate revenue.

Advertising, value-added services, and reselling of network services to government bodies and large organizations are some ways to create the revenue needed to keep the network running. It is also important to recognize that it may be more important to address the sustainability of the improved relationships that rural telecommunication systems help establish, as opposed enhancing only the sustainability of the service itself. By encouraging stakeholders to use rural telecommunication systems to enhance relationships, those relationships will provide the foundations for the sustainability of the system.

Community ownership, management and involvement is important. Centralized telecommunication operators would be wise to decentralize rural service and enable the resale or franchise of service areas to local operators, cooperatives or municipal organizations. The more local the operator, the more likely the system will be responsive to user needs and facilitate sustainable revenues.

Participatory community management will help a network thrive. Community members need mechanisms for influencing network management, system design, and the development of creative and beneficial applications. Local advisory councils can provide a great deal of support and advice to enable local operators to provide beneficial and profitable services.

Provide opportunities for students and young people to learn about the technology and the community development potential of rural telecommunication systems. This too will enhance sustainability and the ability of the rural service to grow to meet needs, while creating new employment opportunities for young people, especially young people living in rural areas.

Strategic marketing brings higher revenues, better service and helps reach rural development objectives. Operators that make an effort to understand specific clients and market services that meet their needs will be rewarded with profits. Train volunteers to train new users. Those of us who are used to using telephones may think that using a telephone requires no training. On the contrary, rural people who have had few chances to use a telephone, or a more sophisticated telecommunication application, will very likely require an orientation period to become comfortable with the tool. Community volunteers can assist in training and orienting those who are least comfortable with the tools.

Share resources, ideas and lessons learned with other rural telecommunication operators, advocates and supporters. Sharing lessons learned will help other rural telecommunication initiatives to find their feet faster. Within many nations, regions and organizations, there often exist telecommunication enthusiasts with influence or decision-making authority who, by virtue of age, wisdom and established credibility can lend significant support to specific development initiatives. These are the "respectable wired elders," because, unlike many of their younger peers, their voices and visions can capture the imaginations of "unwired" politicians, funding agency bureaucrats and private sector benefactors. They are often an untapped resource, but their support can add a fantastic boost to a project.

Enlist the support of organizations with existing outreach networks and presence in rural communities. These organizations might include agricultural extension services, rural health services, rural and agricultural cooperatives and credit banks, farmers' organizations, rural library systems, rural women's organizations and rural youth organizations. Collaborate with radio, newspapers, and television services, both locally and nationally in order to build momentum and support for rural telecommunication initiatives and rural stakeholder awareness and engagement.

Recognize that telecommunication policies seldom contain the elements that actively and effectively enable the creative conditions, ownership models, interconnection agreements, and pricing arrangements that foster rural telecommunication services. Stakeholder engagement is one strategy to help change this if stakeholders can assume policy advocacy roles.

Around the world people are working hard to build rural telecommunication systems. We are witnessing a remarkable convergence of private sector and public sector interests. Rural telecommunication ought to be a win-win situation for all involved. Few rural development projects are able to combine private sector profitability with the achievement of rural development objectives. Few rural development projects have the immense communication and knowledge sharing potential of simple telephone services. Communication for development practitioners and rural telecommunication companies and experts have common interests in facilitating rural development. By working together, they can help achieve both profitable and developmentally appropriate rural telecommunication systems.

3

Communication and Human Development

Human development is the process of enlarging the capabilities, choices and opportunities of people - especially the rural and the poor - to lead a long, healthy and fulfilling life. This process includes the expansion of people's capacity and skills to gain access and control over factors that affect their basic needs. To this end, development concentrates on how to lessen poverty, guarantee food security and ensure availability of safe drinking water and improved sanitation. In the same vein, development efforts with communities focus on increasing their members' income and skills, provision of primary health care and basic education as well as expanding people's ability to participate effectively in economic and political affairs of their societies and nations.

Human development can only be achieved when people are empowered to become critically conscious of their social, economic and physical circumstances and to use their creativity to improve the quality of their lives in a sustainable manner. To become empowered, people need relevant skills, information and knowledge in addition to physical resources and technologies to enable them to improve their circumstances. Participation of people in the decision-making processes that lead to the generation and dissemination of the above is crucial. People's participation in these processes ensures that such decisions are relevant to their circumstances and capabilities. This means that the people must be involved in the joint identification and analysis of their needs, problems and the causes, and contribute actively to the development of policies and strategies to solve the problems or provide for the needs.

In this process, people participate in drawing up action plans and in the strengthening of existing community institutions or the formation of new structures to implement, monitor and evaluate the plans. The outcome is often successful and sustainable because people see the decisions and plans as theirs and strive to ensure their effective implementation. This brand of participation increases people's ability to define their own problems and to mobilize themselves for collective action.

When this level of development is achieved, people become empowered. On their own, they seek additional skills, knowledge and outside assistance when they encounter problems beyond their existing capabilities and resources. They also become more aware of the various external political and socio-economic factors that obstruct the achievement of their goals and often use their newly acquired skills of self-mobilization to tackle these obstacles. Development field staff and extension workers who assist people to learn new ways of thinking and interacting with the complex and changing circumstances in which they live become facilitators of sustainable human development.

The problem, however, is that the rural poor who need to benefit from human development efforts are often beyond easy reach. They are frequently illiterate and have ideas, knowledge and practices shaped by deep-rooted cultural norms, traditions, experiences and values different from the those of development workers. These differences render the task of planning and implementing human development projects and programmes difficult.

Communication for development is an innovative way of reaching and interacting with people more effectively wherever they may be. It is a process of using communication research, approaches, methods, traditional and modern media and materials to facilitate the exchange of information, ideas and knowledge among all the people involved in a development effort. The aim is to facilitate mutual understanding and consensus for action among all stakeholders during every step of the process to ensure the success and sustainability of the development effort.

Communication for development seeks to integrate people's culture, attitudes, knowledge, practices, perceptions, needs and problems in the planning and implementation of development projects and programmes to guarantee that they are effective and relevant. It ensures that information from development agencies is useful and relevant and packaged in ways people will find attractive and understandable. In the same way, people's perceptions and knowledge are rendered in ways that will be comprehensible to development agencies.

Participatory Rural Communication Appraisal (PRCA)

Participatory communication research is the beginning of any successful development process aimed at assisting in the improvement of people's livelihood. To this end, the Southern African Development Community (SADC) Centre of Communication for Development, with the support of FAO, has developed an effective method for starting development efforts with the people: "participatory rural communication appraisal" (PRCA). PRCA is a methodology designed for development field workers and extension staff to enable them to conduct multidisciplinary and participatory communication research as the first step to prepare a communication programme.

The principles, visual tools and techniques of PRCA facilitate the participation of people in identifying problems and appropriate solutions. They also allow people and development workers to reach consensus on actions to be taken within the community. PRCA identifies factors that will help people learn about new ideas, in ways that are easy for them to absorb and that are relevant and attractive. PRCA is a careful mix of elements from such social investigation traditions as participatory approaches, qualitative and quantitative research, as well as ethnography. It also incorporates ideas and techniques from the logical framework approach, advertising and marketing research. Through PRCA, rural people's perceptions, interests, needs, problems, aspirations, traditional communication networks and information requirements can be rapidly discovered. Results of PRCA are used to formulate participatory communication programmes for implementation with rural communities. PRCA has been developed to ensure that communication programmes are firmly rooted in the realities of the rural community in order to encourage the success and sustainability of the development effort. These realities are unearthed through sound research that actively involves the people concerned.

This methodology emerged as an answer to the challenge to develop a communication research approach that involves people as equal partners in studies about their lives and aspirations as opposed to treating them as mere objects of research. PRCA, therefore, provides an opportunity for the sharing of knowledge and experiences between rural communities and development workers until mutual understanding and a plan of action is reached. PRCA is built on the definition of communication that explains it as an interactive process characterised by the exchange of ideas, information, points of view and experiences between persons and groups. In PRCA, communication is a two-way process in which the receiver is also a source with information and ideas to transmit. Passiveness is non-existent in this process because it is a process in which an individual or a group enters into dialogue and mental cooperation with another individual or group until they come to a common awareness and understanding. It is a process in which the two decide on a course of action together. In the context of development work, communication therefore presupposes that all actors are equal.

The methodology has been used for the design of communication programmes for new and ongoing projects. Since it was conceptualised in 1994, PRCA has continued to evolve in response to field realities. Comments and suggestions from international experts, field workers and rural people have helped to shape the approach.

An effective communication programme is based on good research conducted with the people involved in a particular programme. Research methods that are not participatory will not do; hence the development of PRCA. PRCA provides an opportunity for the joint identification and analysis of problems, needs and possible solutions by the development workers and the community. Results of PRCA make it possible to formulate objectives, plan problem-solving communication strategies, select communication approaches, design messages and discussion themes, select media and develop materials. For these to be done properly, a first hand knowledge of the important issues and communication systems of the community is essential.

PRCA is most effective if carried out at the same time the development project is being designed with the community. However, PRCA can be designed and used at any point of the project cycle to formulate a communication programme that will initiate or improve dialogue between development workers and the people involved, ensuring that project aims and activities are relevant to people's needs, problems and capabilities.

PRCA enables the community, with facilitation from development workers or extension staff, to identify and analyse their problems, needs and possible solutions. PRCA tools also assist in the generation and analysis of several other categories of information, materials and issues for the purpose of designing an effective problem-solving communication strategy. The list below is only a guideline and should be expanded or shortened depending on prior experiences with participatory approaches and the objectives of the specific appraisal. In addition to any data obtained from secondary sources, PRCA provides the opportunity for a first hand interaction between the people and the development worker. PRCA enables the development worker, the extension staff and the people to arrive at a mutually acceptable interpretation of the community's problems, needs and solutions as well as its socio-economic and physical characteristics. This is necessary because quite often the way outsiders see the community or the descriptions given about them in books - their norms, values, actions and aspirations - might not correspond to the way the people see themselves and vice versa. Knowledge of the people's situation provides the background and context for the other categories of information that will be revealed by PRCA, including those issues concerning communication. To obtain this knowledge, PRCA must create mutual understanding between the development worker and the people in the community in order to reveal how the people perceive and define their world and reality. PRCA can accomplish this because the tools and techniques of the process can break through the suspicion and conspiracies of silence, diplomacy and courtesy often associated with rural communities.

For instance, during a PRCA in a Zambian village, the team of extension workers and communication specialists continually referred to the people as farmers. Towards the end of the appraisal, when the people were now feeling comfortable with the team, the people revealed that they did not perceive themselves as farmers. The people at this juncture gave the team their own definition of a farmer: a person with a title deed to his land. Since the people tilled their land under the traditional land tenure system, in which all ownership is invested in the chief, they did not see themselves as farmers. The implication was that most recommendations that had been presented to these people were not implemented in the village because they were meant for farmers and the people did not see themselves as farmers.

Even within the community, various groups might have different perceptions of problems and needs as well as the environmental and socio-economic situation of the community. It is therefore essential that different groups in the community are interacted with separately during the PRCA in order to hear their own perceptions of the conditions in the community. This separate interaction becomes even more important in communities where some groups, such as women, are traditionally not allowed to voice their opinions in the presence of other groups, such as men.

Profile of the community

PRCA enables development workers and the people to develop a profile of the community as seen by the different groups in the community. This is possible because the people themselves can use various PRCA visual tools and techniques to describe, map or diagram the information essential for the design of an effective communication strategy.

PRCA reveals traditional and modern information and communication networks and systems within a community and between a community and other communities, external organizations and institutions. The nature of the information transmitted through each network and potential uses can also be identified with PRCA. The attributes of the specific networks and systems preferred by the community can be determined using PRCA tools. It is necessary to map the networks and systems because they are the potential channels for communicating with the community in mass, group or interpersonal modes.

Apart from identifying the communication systems and general socio-economic and environmental situation of the community, PRCA also reveals the people's needs, opportunities, problems and likely solutions as perceived by various groups in the community. These are the most essential building blocks of an effective communication programme. While needs represent the lack of material or human resources the community sees as essential for their welfare, opportunities are skills, knowledge, persons, situations or resources that exist in the community and can be exploited in efforts to improve the people's living conditions. Similarly, problems are the negative undesired factors that constrain or stop communities from achieving their basic needs, and solutions are ways of removing or decreasing the problems. As each of the PRCA tools is used, questions regarding these fundamental issues are identified by the community. Focus group discussions, brainstorming and semi-structured interviews are especially useful in drawing out and articulating the needs, opportunities, problems and solutions.

Since many of these will be revealed in the course of a PRCA, such tools as pair-wise ranking and closed or open scoring are used to prioritize them. Problem trees are then developed to analyse the causes of the priority problems. Perceptions play a major role in defining needs and problems. Ideally, community needs, opportunities, problems and solutions should be identified at the beginning of the project with the participation of the people.

A multisectoral and -disciplinary team should do this so that the people will join in the selection of priorities. However, in reality, the development agency, government ministry or NGO often defines the limits of project formulation research and efforts, prescribing the issues to be paid attention to and their subsequent priorities. For ongoing projects, therefore, the analysis starts from the project's problem statement, mission, and objectives before field PRCA is conducted. This analysis will produce a problem tree based on the project's perceptions of the problems and the causes. During PRCA in the community, the people are also asked to develop their own problem tree on the issue the project is concerned with. The project problem tree is then compared with the peoples' problem tree to find out whether there is mutual understanding or not.

Interaction groups

The term "interaction group", unlike "target group" or "public", presupposes that the people involved are not passive receivers of information, but that they have valuable knowledge, opinions and perceptions. Interaction groups are seen as sources of information, initiators of action, and decision-makers. They can be individuals, associations, agencies, institutions or cooperatives in and outside the community whose activities, needs, problems affect the people in a positive or negative manner.

All communities are made up of different groups: men, women, the literate, the illiterate, etc. Some groups in the community such as the very poor, the outcasts or the sick might be invisible. If the issues under discussion concern such "missing" groups, PRCA seeks them out for dialogue.

PRCA enables the development worker to segment the community in order to select and define the key interaction groups. Segmentation is the art of grouping together people and institutions within and without the community on the basis of their relationship to the identified community needs, opportunities, problems and solutions.

Internal interaction groups are groups of people in the community who share a certain problem or need and people who are potentially in a position to assist in some way in the solution of the problem or provide for the need.

External interaction groups are groups of people or institutions outside the community that have skills, resources, influence or knowledge to assist in the solution of the problems or provision of the needs. These are often development project staff: managers, technical experts, extension workers and policy-makers.

During PRCA, the divisions within the community in relation to the needs, opportunities, problems and solutions become more obvious. This helps to divide the people into more meaningful groups, define their characteristics and design communication strategies that are relevant to them. Information collected provides the basis for identifying the groups who are most seriously affected by the current status of the community or variability in the people's circumstances.

As PRCA defines the general community needs, opportunities, problems and solutions with the people, it also distinguishes between structural and communication needs and problems. Communication alone cannot solve structural needs and problems which often must have material inputs for their solution. Communication problems, on the other hand, can be caused by factors related to either the development agency or the interaction group.

PRCA is therefore used to define the communication issues as they relate to the key interaction groups. By seeking answers to the questions below from the key interaction groups, a better picture of the groups' communication needs begins to appear. Such tools and techniques as the problem tree and focus group discussion are suggested for this exercise. Lack of or low awareness of the problem and possible solution may be due to poor or too little use of communication by the development agencies to raise awareness of the problem in ways people relate to. Solutions, in the same manner, may not have been packaged in ways that bring out their attributes in a persuasive manner to show their relevance to the removal of the problem. Focus group discussions with the various groups will determine their level of awareness of the problems and solutions.

The lack of common understanding of the needs, problems, possible solutions and opportunities between the community and the development agencies is one of the most common communication challenges in projects. For any meaningful progress to be made, the causes and effects of the problems as perceived by the group must be ascertained. Lack of commitment and motivation to tackle a problem can be a communication problem. The people in the community might not see the problem as a priority and in some cases, peer pressure or community norms might discourage people from recognizing the situation as problematic. The mental position or attitude that people have about a problem will often determine how they behave towards it. Some people in the group might decide not to use a technique for solving some problem despite the fact that they have knowledge of it because they do not have a positive attitude towards that technique. It is therefore important to find out people's attitude towards issues under discussion. With such information a communication strategy can be developed to change a negative attitude in order to solve a problem.

Lack of interest or a negative attitude towards an issue is often a result of the inability of the group to try out alternatives in a non-threatening situation. When there are no opportunities for trial of new technologies for instance, people will not be able to judge such technologies in order to decide whether to use them or not. Communities often develop a negative attitude towards an issue as a result of the manner in which the development field workers or extension officers treat the people. Many development workers do not have respect for the people for whom they work. They see the people as inferior and ignorant and the people often sense this. A communication barrier can be created between the two parties when this happens.

Groups can get demoralized by the lack of appropriate policy support from government or development agencies. When issues of concern to the people are neglected at the policy level, there is a tendency for people to neglect such issues unless communication approaches are used to mobilize the community to action. The groups' attitude and level of interest in a particular issue can also be determined through a focus group discussion and the ranking they ascribe to the issue through various PRCA tools, especially the problem tree.

Insufficient information, skills and knowledge to deal with a problem is a common communication problem in many communities. Cultural beliefs and practices can also become barriers to tackling problems even when the knowledge and other requirements for a solution are in place. PRCA will reveal the beliefs of the community in relation to the issues under discussion. Although some of these beliefs might appear as nothing more than superstition, making positive reference to them in the communication materials may determine the success or failure of the communication programme. Knowing the groups' beliefs will provide answers to the question: Why do people make decisions to act in certain ways and on what basis?

Lack of skills and knowledge can also manifest itself if the development agency is producing instructional materials that are difficult for the people to understand or that do not appear relevant to them. To ensure relevance of communication materials, it is essential to identify and utilise local knowledge as an entry point for the new practices. The local knowledge of the community consists of those techniques and practices which are essentially subsistence-oriented, distinct to a particular social group and culture and have been developed and handed down from generation to generation. These are usually built up on centuries of experience and adaptation. Local knowledge is expressed in local languages. They may have been influenced by innovations emerging from within the community or from other systems, but they essentially originated locally. Such knowledge can provide insight into how people normally solved their problems and provided for their needs.

On the other hand, adopted knowledge consists of techniques, processes and practices that were originally introduced into the community from outside. It is essential to assess how much of this knowledge the community actually has. Increasing such knowledge might become an objective of the communication strategy if the level is found to be low. Focus group discussions, in-depth interviews and observation are the suggested tools for studying this aspect of the groups' characteristics.

While finding out all the above information, it is also important to identify with the groups the additional information, knowledge, skills and resources they need in order to solve the problem.

Channels and influential sources of information

With PRCA tools - such as communication resource maps, linkage diagrams, pair-wise preference ranking, direct matrix ranking, scoring, focus group discussions and chapati diagrams - the communication and information networks, systems and channels of the key interaction group(s) can be defined. These tools can be used to reveal the groups' preferred modern and traditional information sources both within and from outside the community. These can range from cultural/religious events, rituals, art, drawings, story telling, dances, songs, role-play, drama, to audio-visual and print media. These tools can also help to identify influential people and institutions the groups see as credible. PRCA helps to identify the idioms, vocabulary, cultural norms and associations, symbols and stories the groups use in discussing the development issues.

PRCA is a participatory and qualitative methodology that can only provide information on what people are doing and thinking, but cannot always quantify how many people in the community are doing or thinking about the same things. Apart from revealing how many people are doing what in the community, the baseline study builds upon the findings of the PRCA to sharpen the objectives of the communication programme and make them measurable during the evaluation that comes at the end of the communication programme.

Communication Skills Development

Skills of PRCA are learnt by participants in The Action Programme for Communication Skills Development, a service of the Southern Africa Development Community's Centre of Communication for Development. It is an integrated and systematic approach to improve the skills of national personnel to plan, implement and manage communication programmes to assist field staff and extension workers for various development purposes.

The Action Programme gives participants the ability and confidence to design and utilise various communication strategies, approaches and media to increase people's participation in new and on-going development projects. The aim is to achieve specific development goals.

The Action Programme imparts skills that enable the participants to define clear and realistic objectives for communication programmes, through participatory appraisal of rural people's problems, needs, opportunities, perceptions, attitudes, knowledge and aspirations.

Participants also learn to design an effective communication strategy that is above all affordable, using local resources, activities, media materials and channels appropriate in rural areas.

The Action Programme enables participants to advise development field staff and extension workers who will help to carry out the planned communication programme on the appropriate utilization of participatory techniques as well as selected communication activities, media materials and channels.

4

Integrated Rural Development through Telecommunications

In countries all around the world, the telecommunication industry is undergoing restructuring, usually with a visible sense of urgency. First, it is increasingly evident that telecommuni-cations and economic development are very closely linked. Intuitively, this seems logical. Scientific investigation and analysis has confirmed that the correlation between telecommunications and economic development is very high. Second, the telecommunication industry in many countries is under-going restructuring because it is now widely realized that the old, rigid "government telecom monopoly model" meets neither the communicating public's needs nor the country's national policy objectives. Under this model, telecommunication services are delivered by a government department run on civil service lines, with political masters and at tariffed rates which are arbitrarily set based on policy and political judgement, without reference to cost structures and commercial reality. The greatest challenge for developing countries is to ensure that telecommunication services, and the resulting benefits of economic, social and cultural development which these services promote, are extended effectively and efficiently throughout the rural and remote areas - those areas which in the past have often been disadvantaged, with few or no telecommunication services.

These rural and remote areas will in fact benefit most from the advent of telecommunications, because alternative methods of passing information are more costly and difficult than in densely populated areas. As a result, without telecommunications the information is either not put forward and the value of it is lost, or it is put forward in some other way, at greater cost or with delay or both.

Telecommunication Industry

It is now well recognized that the telecommunication industry is inherently commercial in nature. The provision of good telecommunication services is an enterprise which can and should be profitable in its own right. Especially in the rural and remote areas, it provides a valuable and vital stimulus for economic growth, and also for social and cultural development.

To release this inherent commercial vigour, some structural adjustment is often necessary. It is important to separate responsibility for:

i) establishing national telecommunications policy;

ii) for regulation of the industry; and

iii) for the actual provision of telecommunication services to customers. Responsibility for national telecommunications policy and regulation of the telecommunications industry continues to be a government responsibility.

Experience has shown that the provision of telecommunication services is carried out most effectively on a commercial basis. The actual ownership of the service providing organization may be the private or public sector, or ownership may be joint. The important thing is that the organization operates, and is judged, as a commercial enterprise.

Experience in many developing countries has shown that the actual operational provision of telecommunication services can often be made substantially more effective and valuable by selective liberalization. The objective of liberalization is to enable and encourage organizations which provide telecommunication services to think and act as business ventures, seeking always to minimize cost and mazimize revenue, to respond quickly and economically to customers' needs, both expressed and anticipated, and to promote the use of the services that are offered, especially those that are the most valuable to the users and profitable to the service providers.

To seize and take advantage of the economic opportunity that telecommunications brings to developing countries, the essential requirement is that the service providers should think and behave with an entrepreneur's mindset, not that of a civil servant.

These days, appropriately, the emphasis in considering rural telecommunications is very much on "applications" - how the telecommunication services will be used; and how, in turn, this usage will benefit the citizens of the region served. Experience indicates that the introduction of sufficient quantities of modern telecommunication services in previously unserved or underserved rural and remote areas stimulates economic development, social development, and cultural development.

Telecommunications enables a whole range of commercial functions to be carried out quickly and easily, functions which previously were at best slow and costly, and at worst could not be carried out at all. Functions now made easier include finding markets for farm produce, fisheries catches and handicraft products, negotiating prices and quantities, arranging for pickup and delivery, and so on. On the input side of commercial enterprises, telecommunications facilitates such functions as arranging for the required factors of production and making arrangements with and for workers. On both the input and the output side of commerce, telecommunications makes it much easier to follow up on contracts, and explore potential business development opportunities.

Telecommunications makes it possible to obtain and to distribute information of all sorts. Databases and other information sources can be accessed, providing information, amongst many other things, on distant markets, market and consumption trends, and future markets.

Telecommunications brings the ability to carry out all sorts of transactions electronically. This includes financial transactions and also information-type transactions. The flow of information in the reverse direction also brings value. The government and other appropriate organizations can now obtain census-type and other statistical information electronically, and, as a result, can improve the quality and timeliness of decision-making and delivery of services. Tourism is a commercial area which is just not feasible without adequate telecommunications, which are essential in developing the business, in promoting it, and in making the reservations and detailed arrangements that this industry requires. Experience indicates that potential tourism customers refuse to go to areas where "reasonable" telecommunications are not available. Tourism is a rapidly expanding industry worldwide, and offers a significant commercial opportunity for many developing countries.

Educational opportunities can be greatly expanded by tele-education, or "distance learning", techniques. There are examples of educational programmes available through telecommunications, that embrace the whole range of education from primary school to university. For many of the residents of the rural and remote areas of developing countries, this capability has the potential to open a broad spectrum of new educational possibilities. In educational applications, a variety of technologies can play a role.

Often, the transmission arrangement is asymmetric, the transmission medium providing both images and voice from the teacher to the students, with only voice response from student to teacher. Pedagogically, this arrangement has been found to work well. Telemedicine is an active and expanding field. Good quality data service capability is necessary so that medical readings and records and files can be transmitted reliably. Now, instead of having to move either the patient to the doctor or vice versa, it becomes possible to move only the relevant medical information. As well as direct patient care, experience has demonstrated that valuable telemedicine applications include in-service coaching and training of remote-located health care staff. In embracing an entrepreneurial approach to the provision of telecommunication services, the promotion of services, in particular the high revenue/high margin services, is an important opportunity to be pursued. International long distance calling, which has been increasing dramatically worldwide for several years, is an important and profitable example. The experience of many developing countries indicates that there are significant numbers of expatriates who are living in other countries who want to keep in touch with, the family and friends that they have left behind in the rural villages. Nor is it necessary for these calls to be paid for by the citizens in the rural and remote areas.

Telecommunications makes possible timely and effective communication between the rural population and government departments and agencies, in ways that were previously not possible. Telecommunications makes it possible for the government to warn of impending natural hazards, for example hurricanes. If and when disasters occur, the government is able to quickly provide appropriate aid with maximum effectiveness and with economy of effort, because it is now possible to determine with precision the necessary kinds of aid, to be brought to precisely where it is needed. Less dramatic but actually of greater value is the ongoing non-emergency communication between government organizations and the rural and remote areas.

In the environmental field, for example, information about good environmental practices can be provided to the citizens, and they, in turn, can notify the central organization of possible adverse situations so that these situations can be dealt with before they become a problem. Effective communications is a vital tool in countering threats to personal safety and to national security. Such threats could come from the criminal element, or possibly even from terrorist organizations. Through telecommunications, the security forces can be notified and summoned, can monitor events as they unfold, and can take appropriate action to enforce the rule of law. Telecommunications play an important role in democratic processes; for example in elections. Information about the election is distributed throughout the rural areas. Those responsible for managing and supervising the electoral procedures do this using telecommunications. Local election results are reported to central locations via telecommunications, and overall national election results flow back the other way. The advent of telecommunications in the rural and remote areas provides an opportunity to extend to these areas government services and capabilities that previously were not provided because of prohibitive costs.

It has been found that the practical and economically viable way to deliver telecommunication services in the rural and remote areas of developing countries is by providing a group of lines that provide access to the telecommunication services at a convenient central location within each rural community. This approach is experienced based and commercially driven. The upkeep costs, operations and maintenance, of isolated loop networks are high, since these networks have above-average trouble experience and repair visits are time consuming.

The service provider's goal is to maximize revenue earned in the community. Since charges are based on usage, long calls should be encouraged. A line of people waiting to obtain a line is a clear sign of inadequate provisioning. Also, inward calls, generally originating in another country, are a valuable source of revenue. An event that should never happen is that an international call progresses all the way to the rural village, and then finds no line available to complete the connection.

Other advantages of centralizing the telecommunication services in the community include ready support for users in using the service, at least some basic maintenance capability, ease of ensuring the security of both the service and the equipment, and easy provisioning of the required power. Last but certainly not least, charges for service usage can be collected on the spot, and debit cards can be sold in advance of the actual usage.

As the needs of the community warrant, more capability and capacity must be added. This could well include transaction capability, both financial and data oriented, and the ability to access remote databases. Not specifically a telecommunication service but related to it, copying capability and the provision of personal computers equipped with modems to enable data transmission for hire will be valuable assets. Audio conferencing, perhaps with the ability to also transmit text-type material, and eventually video conferencing, will fill out the portfolio of offered telecommunication services.

Principles for providing telecommunications

There continue to be substantial areas of many countries with little or no telecommunications to serve the inhabitants. Noting that telecommunications is inherently a commercial enterprise, and a potentially profitable one, and recognizing the close linkage between telecommunications and economic, social and cultural development, high priority should obviously be given to providing good telecommunication services where they are not now available.

Universal access

Access to telecommunication facilities and services will be provided at a convenient central location in each community. The portfolio of services offered will meet the needs of the community. Both the types and quantity of services offered will increase as demand grows, and new applications and opportunities emerge.

Rural telecommunications will be introduced through a carefully planned, well-structured and managed, rigorous and orderly multiyear programme. Experience indicates that this approach will obtain the lowest prices and the best support from vendors of network systems and equipment. Also, as the programme progresses, the operator's personnel will gain valuable experience and will "move up the learning curve". As a result, the programme will become progressively more effective and efficient, and internal costs per line added will drop dramatically. This approach offers the opportunity to negotiate substantially lower equipment prices. The required support arrangements, e.g., tools and test sets, training the operations and maintenance staff, and provision of maintenance spares, become a much smaller proportion of the total cost. For obvious commercial reasons, the programme should start in those rural areas which are expected to have the greatest service demand, and to be the most profitable. The prospectively "least profitable - highest loss" areas will be served last. As effectiveness and efficiency improve, the costs of network extension will go down, probably dramatically. These last areas will be served when the programme expertise is highest and costs are a minimum. As a result, these areas may in fact prove to be profitable. If they are unprofitable, they will be only marginally so. Experience indicates that the successful planning, organization and management of the rural telecommunications programme is a very important factor in creating a cost-effective rural telecommunications infrastructure that provides a service which can be priced low enough to be widely used, and hence valuable to the residents, and yet is profitable and sustainable.

An appropriate regulatory framework will be required, which creates the necessary terms and conditions to promote the initial provision and continuing sustainability of the rural service. A firmly enunciated "universal service obligation" of the service provider, to serve the rural and remote areas and defining how the obligation will be measured, is usually necessary. Conditions addressed by the regulatory framework will certainly include interconnection and revenue settlement. The revenue settlement arrangement should be based on legitimate causal costs. Simple schemes such as sender keeps all typically disadvantage the rural service provider substantially, and for this reason are not satisfactory. The regulatory agency must monitor the sustained availability, quality and financial viability of the rural service, preferably through aggregated versions of the same indicators that the service provider uses for his own internal management requirements. Despite the service provider's best efforts, a modest subsidy may be appropriate in fulfilling the universal service obligation. The subsidy should be as low as is consistent with ensuring the continued sustain-ability of the rural service. The operator's success in pursuit of com mercial principles is a key factor in minimizing the level of support.

It is important that funds that are already in the service provider's hands should be permitted to remain in the service provider's hands, for reinvestment in the network. This may require changes in legislation at the national level; for example, to encourage investment in the network, the government may very wisely specify that earnings will not be taxed if they are reinvested in the network.

For investment funds to be forthcoming from potential private sector investors, it is essential that the rural telecommunications network must be expected to be, and in practice must be seen to be, a profitable enterprise.

The final principle underlies the other four. The rural telecommunications network must be operated as a commercial, entrepreneurial, profit-focused and profitable enterprise. It is this "mind set" that will motivate the service provider to continually seek to maximize revenues and minimize costs. There are many opportunities to do this. As telecommunication services are progressively provided throughout the rural and remote areas, the commercial challenge is to operate the network and the services effectively, efficiently, and profitably.

In the rural telecommunications context, this would include such things as hours of business, general physical arrangements, a standard franchise agreement, standard financial accounting and reconciliation arrangements, and standard operations and basic maintenance procedures for the telecommunications equipment.

Within this supportive framework and set of guidelines and practices, the franchise holder adapts the operation to best meet the needs of the residents. The franchise holder is a local resident, and hopefully is viewed as a helpful and dedicated pillar of the local business community. He or she benefits financially by operating the franchise effectively. Motivating financial arrangements, for example payment to the franchise holder based on percent of revenue, are typical of franchise operations, and are very suitable. Effective franchise operation involves continuing, detailed results-oriented management of the franchise holders by the franchise granting organization.

Rural Networking Cooperatives

Today, advances in networking technologies provide some unique opportunities for developing countries. To expand their trading opportunities, for example, developing countries can use high-speed broadband networks to link up to foreign markets. Similarly, low cost networked information technologies, such as the Internet, can be used to facilitate political and community participation. Equally important, social services - such as health care and education - can now be provided via satellite on a much more cost-effective basis.

Recognizing this potential, many developing countries are poised to make major investments in communication infrastructure in the hope of fostering economic development and facilitating the integration of their markets into a knowledge-based global economy. Foreign assistance organizations are similarly considering telecommunications-related programmes to reduce the costs and enhance the benefits of providing foreign aid.

The time is certainly ripe to make such investments. Networking technology costs are plummeting, while their performance is improving phenomenally. Soon these technologies will be essential, given an increasingly information-based and electronically networked global economy. Countries that take advantage of these technologies will gain competitive advantages, while countries that fail to recognize their potential, or who cannot gain access to these technologies, will probably experience decline. In developing countries, advanced communication technologies can play a special role. These technologies not only allow countries to leapfrog to a modern infrastructure; they can also serve as a catalyst, helping to promote social and economic behaviour more conducive to development.

Although recent advances in communication technologies hold promise to improve political and economic conditions in developing countries, the realization of this promise is far from certain. As history bears witness, the evolution of technologies is replete with disappointments and unintended consequences. Success will depend not only on assuring the supply and deployment of advanced networks; of equal, if not more, importance will be the social, economic, and political context in which these technologies are deployed. If, for example, developing countries do not have the requisite skills and expertise, they will be unable to employ networking technologies to their best advantage. Equally important, if developing country leaders use communication technologies solely to perpetuate their own control, or to reinforce unproductive practices, technology deployment may serve to make countries worse off. If networking technologies are to promote development, deployment strategies must be integrated with complementary social and economic policies that address the full range of development barriers.

Designing a technology diffusion strategy to meet social as well as economic criteria will, however, be particularly difficult in an increasingly deregulated, global economic environment in which the political and economic modus operandi is to let the market take it course. For developing countries, the task is especially troublesome. Lacking capital and deeply in debt, many countries must depend on foreign investment for their telecommunications infrastructure development. Although such investment will surely be forthcoming, its provision will be based almost exclusively on market criteria. Thus, developing countries will need to fine tune their strategies, focusing on specific market failures and socio-economic contexts, in order to create appropriate economic incentives to ensure that technology deployment and diffusion is consistent with their broader development goals.

The experience of the rural telephone cooperatives in the United States provides an example of one type of strategy that might be pursued. These cooperatives were highly successful in developing innovative ways to provide affordable telephone services to the many rural communities in the United States that were unserved by the marketplace. Building upon, and reinforcing, the strengths of their own communities, they played a critical role not only in promoting the universal deployment of communication technologies and services, but also their widespread use in support of economic and community development.

Although countries differ considerably in terms of their social, economic and political contexts, the rural cooperative model has a universal appeal. In fact, this model has proved to be so versatile that it continues to serve today as the basis for providing rural Internet access in many United States communities. Networked information technologies can have far-reaching consequences. They not only affect relationships of time and space; they also help to structure social and economic organization as well as values. Thus, if networked information technologies are to serve developing country development needs, it is not enough to have timely access. Equally if not more important, these technologies must be designed for the task at hand, and deployed and diffused in a manner that supports and reinforces development goals.

Telecom strategies that support and reinforce comprehensive, holistic development approaches, and that focus on the most remote and poorest rural communities, are likely to have especially high pay-off in this regard. It is in rural communities that the barriers to development are most pronounced, with problems in one area typically spilling over and feeding on those in others. The result is a vicious circle that spirals downward. To reverse this pattern requires a concerted community effort which addresses all these structural problems, at one and the same time. Only by adopting such a multifaceted approach will the solution be mutually reinforcing as well.

Community-based actions can also help reinforce a spirit of cooperation and the development of a civil society, upon which democracy and economic development ultimately depend. At the same time, the mobilization of a community and/or community-based organizations can help encourage entrepreneurship and build local competence, thus providing a powerful counter-weight to authoritarian governments and other vested interests opposed to social and economic change. Telecommunications based development strategies are well suited to support such a decentralized, holistic approach. Because communications is essential to all activities, networks can be employed for multipurposes, giving rise to many positive synergies and externalities. As a result, such networks can often sustain themselves in a market economy, complementing rather than competing with networks being deployed under more competitive conditions in higher density areas. If, however, public support is required, it can be both comprehensive and cost-contained. Similarly, small-scale pilot projects can be undertaken and deployment strategies can be most easily adapted to, and brought into line with, actual social, economic, and political conditions. At the same time, telecommunications projects can be customized to build on and take advantage of "local knowledge." Tailoring diffusion strategies to meet local needs is critical, because all too often infrastructure projects in developing countries deteriorate over time given a failure to transfer technological expertise and promote local entrepreneurship.

Rural phone companies organized themselves in a wide variety of ways. Some purely private companies, which functioned as intercom systems, consisted of a single line, which was owned and shared by a small group of people. Others were organized on a profit-seeking basis as privately owned and commercial stock companies. Mutual stock companies, in contrast, were owned entirely by users; organized on an informal basis, their members paid a prorated share of the capital expenditures, maintenance, and improvement fees.

Rural phone companies were able to make do with limited resources by keeping their expenses to a minimum. Local farmers, for example, often built networks using their own materials and tools. When neces-sary, they purchased equipment from independent manufacturers or through mail order catalogues distributed by such firms as Sears and Roebuck and Montgomery Ward. The rapid diffusion of telephone service in rural areas was a measure of its value to users. Because of their remote locations, rural communities derived great benefit from the telephone. People used the phone to summon doctors, visit one another, obtain weather reports, learn about sales in towns, and keep abreast of prices. Whereas the telegraph and mass media technologies had directed local community attention outward, most telephone conversations were local in nature.Despite their initial successes and the important service benefits that they provided, the rural telephone companies' fates were inextricably linked to those of the communities that they served. With industrialization and the onset of the Great Depression, they were increasingly unable to sustain themselves. This trend was only reversed when the Federal Government decided to adopt a less market oriented, and more community-based, approach to telephone deployment in rural areas. Rural electric cooperatives also played an important role in economic development. The cooperatives aggressively recruited and served industrial, commercial, and suburban customers, which had the effect of increasing the number of consumers each year.

The contribution of the Rural Electrification Administration to rural America was by no means limited to technology deployment, however. By educating and working jointly with rural telephone companies, REA fostered technology transfer without which the local telephone systems could not have been upgraded and maintained. In addition, by channelling its support to local providers, who relied as much as possible on local resources, the REA helped to reinforce rural economies. This policy, in turn, had positive cumulative effects. Because the independent and cooperative telephone companies were socially embedded in their local communities, their managers and owners were able to quicken the flow of market information and pass on their technical skills and entrepreneurial expertise. Moreover, in cases where telephone providers were organized as cooperatives - which operated according to democratic principles - the process of managing and administering the provision of telephone services help to build the "social capital" that can greatly facilitate economic development in a rural environment.

Today, many rural communities in the United States are not much better situated for the diffusion of the Internet than they were a half a century ago for the diffusion of the telephone. Although differing from one another significantly, most rural towns and communities continue to suffer from poverty, sparse populations, thin markets, low levels of investment, out-migration, and underdeveloped human resources. To overcome the barriers to the diffusion of the Internet, many local telephone providers are pursuing the same cooperative, community-based strategies that served them well in the past. Central to their approach is a focus on community, the sharing of resources, and an emphasis on education and technology transfer.

As in the past, rural independent telephone companies and cooperatives rely on the support of one other to help them overcome the high cost and complexity entailed in providing rural Internet services. Where there were no formal consortia, other kinds of joint service arrangements were generally established. Thus, to avoid the high capital investment for routers, servers, modems and transport, many rural providers have become secondary Internet service providers. Accordingly, under a variety of configurations, a rural telephone company or cooperative might purchase access from a primary provider and repackage it under its own name as a dial up service or a dedicated access service. In addition, it might outsource customer support and billing services, while doing all of the advertising and marketing itself.

Overcoming the problems of cost and complexity for themselves has been only half the battle for rural telecommunication providers; to promote the Internet, they have also had to help users cope with the many difficulties entailed in Internet usage. This level of support is not surprising, given the nature of the Internet. Unlike the telephone, which was relatively inexpensive and easy to use, the Internet is both costly and complex. Just to get started, a user must purchase, install, and learn how to use a computer - tasks that are by no means trivial. Rural cooperative and independent telephone companies have also helped to educate users through their marketing efforts. Most provide some kind of user training especially to their local schools and libraries. Some have gone so far as to provide "house calls." In addition, a number of companies have provided periodic newsletters or other announcements reporting on Internet developments and what's new on the Web. By packaging Internet information with local news, local telephone companies have made it easier for their customers to relate to it.

This type of close relationship between local providers and customers is mutually reinforcing. Explaining his company's eagerness to work with community schools, one rural cooperative manager said, for example, that such collaboration provided an excellent way to gain the "networking" experience required to expand beyond providing mere "dial-up" access. Rural customers who have little experience dealing with large telecommunications and computer companies can also gain from "knowing" their community providers. Local providers not only are more knowledgeable about local needs, they are also more likely than distant providers to be "on-call," and accountable for the quality of their services.

The broad applicability of the cooperative model has typically been limited, however, by a number of factors. Given, for example, the rising cost and growing size and complexity of networks, it became increasingly difficult to piece together at the local level all of the necessary financial and human resources necessary to create a community-based telephone system. Network interdependencies and the need for interconnections also favoured centralized network ownership and administration, essentially foreclosing the option of a decentralized, cooperative approach.

In today's global, more privatized environment there are few such constraints, however. Taking advantage of the higher performance and enhanced variety of new communication technologies as well as the much greater flexibility that they afford new networking solutions can be employed to deploy communication technologies on an ad hoc and customized basis. In developed countries, large businesses were the first to pursue this strategy by creating private networks to meet their own, specialized needs. Given the possibility of technology leapfrogging, there is no reason why developing countries cannot employ a similar approach to serve users in small communities and rural areas. Already, many countries are deploying less costly communication systems. In other countries, such as India, fixed cellular radio systems are often used. These radio-based systems are easier to deploy than wireline services, and they have lower up-front investment costs, which can be shared among subscribers. They can, moreover, be deployed on a step-by-step basis, with new cells added in response to growing demand. Because radio technology is more reliable, such systems also have lower costs of maintenance.

Given their potential to strengthen local communities, one problem that may arise in establishing bottom-up networks is a political one. If, for example, governments in developing countries continue to jealously guard their monopolies, community networks may lack the means for interconnection with the public switched network. This possibility may be less likely in the future, however, because of the trends towards liberalization and privatization. But if rural communities are faced with such situations, some mutually advantageous arrangements will need to be worked out. National providers might agree, for example, to franchise the development of portions of the network to rural communities. And, if necessary, agreements might be made to allow national providers or privatized monopolies to subsequently acquire rural networks in exchange for some type of equity ownership. Foreign aid policies might be designed to encourage such arrangements as well.

Global cooperative networks

Reflecting the growing appreciation of the role communication technologies can play in fostering economic development, there are today a number of forces promoting its greater diffusion. These activities are both public and private, national and multinational, trade-related and aid related. As in the case of the cooperatives themselves, policies that are designed to leverage all these complementary forces are bound to be the most cost effective. Equally important, they will probably have a synergistic effect resulting from many positive externalities. Communication and economic development serve not only to foster one another, they also feed on themselves.

Achieving Viable Rural Service

Some countries are demonstrating that privatization can be harnessed to bring about very significant improvements in the level of telephone and telecommunications services in rural areas. With a liberalized environment and with falling costs from developments in wireless technology, the envelope for commercial supply has broadened considerably. Some policy makers have helped to "push the envelope" by forcing or encouraging privatized operators to include a major rural element in their build programmes, or by offering market entry opportunities for operators who will focus specifically on rural areas. However, the achievements to date are only a fraction of the total needs of rural areas and of the potential market.

The fact that the public interest - the optimal flow of potential socio-economic benefits - is often not realized unless the operator is motivated and committed to providing a decent level of service, is a pivotal policy issue. It is argued that socio-economic benefits, financial revenues and commercial viability go hand in hand and that the role of policy is to create an environment which will encourage private investment as far as possible.

It is therefore in both the public and private interest to find an enlightened policy mix which will blend commercial incentive and socio-economic demands, in order to bring about further accelerations in rural service investments. The role and features of two discrete rural telecom investment models, namely monopoly internal cross-subsidization and special regional operators. Specific policy requirements are addressed and suggestions are made on ways in which rural network expansion can be accelerated on a commercial basis even more.

Policy makers have a unique opportunity. Most are agreed that with sector reform, the provision of services to rural and low income areas must receive special attention, to ensure that rural areas are included in the benefits of sectoral reform. On all continents, the extension of rural telephone service is being stimulated by means of imposed operator obligations, by new entry opportunities and by special licensing conditions.

The public interest is to secure the social and economic benefits of the telephone and, increasingly, access to information services for all sectors and regions. In the late 1990's, we are no longer asking what these benefits are, but rather how can we be sure they are realized. If the first condition is not universally true, the second one is all too common. The important factor to remember is that the socio-economic benefits from telecommunications, just like revenues, are primarily call dependent.

For every call made, the user pays a fee and also derives a "consumer surplus" - an economic benefit in the form of cost savings over other ways of communicating, or a social or economic benefit from new opportunities and "connectedness" not enjoyed before. But if the service is poor, calls are fewer than they could be and operator revenues do not reach potential. The likelihood of financial loss increases, while at the same time the social and economic impact goes largely unrealized, or at least is sub-optimal. Rural telecommunications have endured this unfortunate cycle for too long. They have been labelled as unprofitable and given subsidies, while the organizations responsible to mobilize the subsidized resources have been insufficiently motivated to optimize either their network designs or their operational modalities.

Enforced internal cross-subsidization

When monopoly operators or concession holders are forced or enticed to provide a minimum level of rural access or to include a certain percentage of rural lines in their build programme they are, in the eyes of many, being required to absorb and "bury" a loss-making component into their programme. Although telephones are deployed, the service may not necessarily be operated in a commercially optimal fashion if it is perceived to be unprofitable.

In the Latin American "monopoly obligation" cases, national or regional monopolies were essentially expected to pay for their privileged status. They were vital, laudable and very significant requirements, although probably looked upon by the operators as costly but acceptable payments for being able to enjoy national or regional monopoly status for the initial period. The Indian new entrants, the Indonesia KSO operators and the Philippine cellular operators are also required to serve rural areas. Their obligations are another form of enforced cross-subsidization.

The cross-subsidization concept has, of course, provided significant improvements in rural access, though one major limitation is that the obligations may reach the commercially most attractive communities at the expense of leaving the most challenging cases still to be served by other means.

Another problem with most internal cross-subsidization strategies is that little attention may be given to optimizing the operational performance and revenue generating capacity of the rural services. While the operator may have few incentives to optimize the service because other parts of the network provide more lucrative returns, a growing body of data from around the world indicates surprising revenue potential from well operated rural systems, including substantial incoming revenues which usually go largely unrecognized in the financial reckoning.

Finally, the internal cross-subsidization model may not provide much preparation for the operation of rural services in a multioperator or competitive environment. Mexican authorities appear to be undecided, as yet, on what obligations can reasonably be placed on new competitive basic service entrants, in order to leverage the next stage of sector reform for the benefit of rural areas.

Defining the Commercial Opportunity

The typical cost/revenue situation for many rural areas is illustrated below. Whereas the first lines in remote areas may be unviable or need to be financed under special provisions because of their high cost, a well-planned wide-area supply strategy using the most appropriate technology can often reduce per-line costs to the point where the potential revenues from supplying a limited number of subscribers in each community exceed costs. Profitability can thus exist if the operator focuses on high revenue lines first, and expands service only as marginal costs and revenues allow. Both the average annual cost of supply and per-line revenue decrease rapidly with the quantity of lines supplied. Hence, a careful balance between demand and supply must be maintained.One of the main challenges for policy makers is to incorporate commercial realities into a coherent framework. Viable operations are able to attract private equity and loan finance. However, rural telecommunications provision has had a hard time because the business case has appeared to be unattractive. Rural service can be profitable within a certain envelope, though the limits of the conventional business case must be recognized. The limits will be less constraining to investment and growth if the regulatory machinery is present to:

— identify and calculate the true incremental revenues and costs attributable to a range of different rural operations (identifying both the rural and urban segments of call completion), setting appropriate and affordable access/penetration obligations accordingly;

— facilitate and monitor the interconnect agreements, revenue splitting or analytical framework (including justification for other incentives such as tax breaks, loans and development fund support) which will provide the enhanced revenue flow operators need if they are to be attracted to invest and to be viable over a wider geographic-economic envelope;

— enforce rural investment targets on monopoly operators which at least correspond to the limits justifiable on the basis of the bothway revenue analysis (i.e., the true financial flows generated).

Even in a single operator environment, operators could be required by financiers to apply a cost-causality and both-way revenue analysis to determine the true financial benefit-to-cost relationship of rural network investment.

This would shift the basis for rural investments from the traditional cross-subsidization argument to one of distributing the full incremental revenues and costs and would be much more palatable to financiers, including development banks.

Whereas the provision of basic service to the most remote and low income communities and regions could still need concessional "development fund" support or cross-subsidization from the more highly profitable services, these situations should be identified and financed as required. It is important to recognize first the full extent of the commercial envelope and to create an environment which provides a non-subsidized and dynamic investment climate to the maximum extent possible.

When we consider the needs of rural areas today, the issue is not whether the telecommunications sector can compete with water, agricultural, health or education projects for aid finance. There is little need for this question to be asked, because telecommunications is a potentially healthy sector in virtually every country. With some policy boldness, the sector can meet almost all of its own service coverage challenges through a combination of creative mechanisms. In doing so, it can benefit every other sector of economic and social activity along the way, without burdening the economy for scarce resources. Demand exists, costs are reducing and innovation brings new possibilities continually. But the lowest cost, lowest risk urban and international markets will attract all of the investments unless the scales are tipped to attract investors into rural service provision. Policy makers have the opportunity and responsibility to influence the investment parameters and create an environment which is favourable to rural telecommunications.

Whether rural areas are served monopolistically or competitively, there are strong arguments for the licensing of special rural operators who will focus specifically on the needs of rural communities. On balance, this is most likely to create a responsive mode of service. In cases where the blend of costs, calling pattern and preferred tariff structure do not allow profitability on a strictly rural basis, regional operators having within their territory both urban and adjacent rural markets can be viable so long as the terms of the interconnect agreement with the national carriers are fair.

In order to assist with attracting and channelling investments into rural areas on a priority basis, policy makers can also use the prize of future market opportunitiesas an enticement. For example, the offering of rural operating licenses or concessions as a means of enabling foreign operators to gain a foothold into the basic services market prior to expiry of the dominant national operator's monopoly would provide a means for them to position themselves for more profitable ventures further on.

All operators should have clear obligations to meet, and should be offered carefully crafted interconnect agreements and incentives which facilitate commercial viability and, wherever possible, long term market sustainability. If this can be achieved, then rural and remote telecom investments could accelerate significantly.

Participatory Communication and Training to Rural Telecentres

Significant sums are being invested by governments, donors, com-munities, non-governmental organizations (NGOs) and the commercial private sector in the deployment of new information and com-munication technologies. There is widespread belief that while information and communication technologies (ICTs) are a "new social and economic force in the world economy," their adoption and utilization in developing countries are constrained by, among other problems, inadequate infrastructure, limited human resource capacity, absence of national policies and low ICT literacy.

In the rush to "wire" developing countries, little attention has been paid to conceptual frameworks or guidelines for ICT utilization, inviting the risk that attempts to introduce ICTs will ignore lessons from past technology transfer efforts, especially those involving information and communication technologies. As with past technologies, ICTs do not in themselves guarantee benefits to local people. In our enthusiasm for ICT technologies and their potential, we should not forget that the focus should be on people, organizations and processes rather than on the technologies themselves. ICTs will not fulfil their potential for rural development unless the special characteristics of the technologies are combined with applications, which focus on participatory communication and training methodologies.

Telecentres that employ ICTs are a relatively recent phenomena. More recently, and on a limited scale, they have been established in developing countries. Such facilities are called a number of names, including "virtual village halls," "telelearning centres," and "telecottages". Telecentres may employ a number of types of ICTs and offer services such as access to telephones and fax machines, photocopiers, printing equipment, e-mail, the Internet and electronic networking. Telecentres are also a venue in which new ICTs, such as the Internet, can interface with conventional ICTs (print, radio and video). The Internet is relatively cheap, powerful, decentralized and potentially an ideal platform to build a flexible and powerful environment for sharing and learning. The Internet is the first communication tool that allows every user to be a sender, receiver, narrowcaster and broadcaster in a global sphere. The nature of the Internet suggests it could be an effective tool for development, and the success of telecentres in Europe suggests that telecentres may be an effective mechanism for making the Internet and other ICTs available to rural communities.

The provision of access to ICTs by rural communities in developing countries is likely to go through telecentres. The purpose of these considerations is to ensure that this development is as effective, efficient, sustainable and equitable as possible, so that the promise of the technology becomes a reality - a tool in the hands of rural people.

When selecting locations for telecentres, consideration should be given to the level of potential demand for communication and information services from a large number and a wide range of users. This will ensure utilization of the facility and reduce the expense to individuals through cost sharing. The proximity of the telecentre to other organizations and institutions that can play roles in using, supporting, maintaining or operating the telecentre should be investigated. Such organizations might include: hospital health centres, schools/colleges/universities, community and cultural centres, religious centres, libraries, organizations of farmers/fishermen/craftsmen, post offices, local/national government administration offices, radio and television stations, NGOs and community-based organizations, among others.

Infrastructural considerations should include: a location that is easily accessible to potential users ; the availability of an existing structure or a new structure which is suited to use as a telecentre; access to electricity; and connection to telephone lines and the Internet. In some situations the development of telecentres may be inappropriate, and other types of communication solutions, electronic or otherwise, should be explored. Socio-cultural aspects that may affect the utilization of the telecentre, or which groups within the community have access to the telecentre, should be investigated. To be effective, telecentres need to be integrated into communities so that they lessen instead of widen the communication gaps between the information rich and the information poor. As in the case of other communication media, the advocates of Internet and other ICTs for development need to look beyond the technologies "to the social and economic systems in which the media function and how these systems influence media access, exposure and impact". In this context, it is important to pay attention to the communication gaps that often exist based on gender, and incorporate into telecentre organization the differential communication patterns that exist between men and women.

A participatory needs assessment can help to identify the information and training requirements of the local population. At the same time, it is important to uncover local skills and knowledge. These two items will help guide the selection and development of applications and help make the technology useful and appropriate for local people. Good techniques for these kinds of assessment, such as participatory rural appraisal (PRA) tools, have already been developed and can be selected according to specific situations. The time required for the assessment will vary depending on factors such as the availability of existing information about the proposed telecentre location, the depth of information required in the planning stage of the telecentre, and the level of use of ICTs at the proposed location.

As a strategy, communication for development can mobilize people for action, promote coordination and linkages among groups and stimulate awareness of, planning for and participation in development. As a strategy for ICT applications, communication for development "begins with the needs of people in rural communities and grassroots agricultural organizations and works to establish vertical and horizontal channels of communication". Through dialogue and consultation, communication can facilitate participatory problem analysis and development planning; it can ensure information flows among concerned groups and promote local information networks; it can link rural knowledge and information systems and help integrate indigenous and scientific knowledge; and it can empower local people to take control of their own development processes.

A good understanding of local communication patterns and processes is essential for telecentre development to ensure appropriate applications of technologies and content to the local situation and for harmonization and integration with existing communication channels and processes. This includes cultural and social norms, where and how people communicate, what is communicated, and by whom. This information can be collected at the same time as the local needs and skills assessment.

"Cyberspace" as a whole can be seen as an ideal platform to build a flexible and powerful environment for sharing and learning. Electronic mail is a uniquely discursive communication mechanism, which can break barriers of time and place. The World Wide Web is a powerful tool for collaboration and participation. At the same time, interactive multimedia applications are redefining publishing and "reading". The cultural impact of ICTs has been demonstrated in business, education, public and private life. However, information and communication technologies are new to many people in rural areas. To assist rural people to identify what technological applications, services and content they may need or want, they will have to be familiar with the uses of the technologies and the potential applications and content appropriate for their situations. Familiarity with the technologies will enable the end users to have a productive dialogue with the designers and suppliers of the applications and to adapt and create their own content. Ways to accomplish this are study tours, which take rural people to where the technologies already exist and/or organizing demonstrations of and training with the technologies in rural areas.One of the greatest risks in telecentre development is that the technology will remain "alien" to the local community and they will feel little involvement or ownership of the telecentre. This of course limits effectiveness and sustainability of the initiative. This can be addressed by engaging the local community in all stages of development of the project and by capacity building which develops the skills of local people to take responsibility for the organization, maintenance and operation of the telecentre.

Applications that could be available in telecentres include "generic" content developed outside the community, however the most important applications are likely to be those which are developed specifically for and by the local users. Many segments of the community should be included in the development of specialised applications, including youth and women. The "generic" applications, which are provided for use in telecentres should, where possible, include functions that allow local communities to contribute their own information to the pool of knowledge.

Telecentres are not just technology centres; they can also be living laboratories, which facilitate local sharing of information and ideas. A telecentre can take full advantage of global information as well as facilitate the creation of a common local development vision. Telecentres are not only a way to provide simple, single-point access to external information and services, but also a facility for local residents and groups to organize village meetings, video conferences and technology training to address their development needs.

Although the emphasis in developed countries has been on the personal computer and personal access to the Internet, this situation is not feasible in rural areas of the developing world at present. Therefore, the link between ICTs and the local people will most likely have to be made through existing communication channels, such as extension agents, NGO workers and rural teachers. Attention to creating and sustaining these linkages will be crucial to ensure that ICTs reach their potential as tools for development. In this regard, it is important to direct attention to how telecentre infrastructure and technology can best be configured or organized to facilitate group use. As well as linkages between the technology and people, there are potentially new interfaces between electronic and non-electronic media and processes. Creative ways of combining the two media will help to increase the effectiveness of both.

Training

Training will be necessary at all stages of telecentre projects. For example, ongoing training will be necessary for the users of the telecentres and periodical training will be required on an as-needed basis to upgrade skills as the technology and content requirements change. Rural colleges and schools, as well as extension services, can use telecentres for professional training, as a facility for distance learning and for farmer tele-training.

When designing training, the users' requirements and learning preferences should be considered, which means that the content and method of delivery should be developed in collaboration with the learners. In addition, training-of-trainers will be necessary to ensure that the training methods and the content of the training sessions they conduct are current and appropriate.

Participatory monitoring and evaluation

It is necessary to monitor and evaluate the process of telecentre development and implementation. The elements monitored should not only include the number of users and the telecentre services that are most utilised, but also the impact of the telecentre on the quality of life in rural areas. Participatory methodologies should be used.

On the basis of monitoring and evaluation, modifications will need to be made in the mode of operation, the services provided and the technology used at the telecentre, because all of these will evolve over time. Although this is true for many projects, it is particularly pertinent to telecentres which employ new and rapidly changing ICTs.

Global Information Infrastructure: The Rural Challenge

In 1984, the International Telecommunication Union's Maitland Commission noted that telecommunications was a "missing link" in much of the developing world. A decade later, policy makers were calling for a "global information infrastructure" that would link everyone into a worldwide network, or more likely, network of networks. Yet a majority of individuals and whole communities in the developing world still do not have access to telecommunications. And where telecommunication facilities exist in developing regions and remote parts of the industrialized world, limited capacity and unreliability may leave users decades behind their better-equipped counterparts who are able to take advantage of converging technologies and new services.

Although there has been a dramatic increase in telecommunication investment in the past decade, there are still enormous gaps in accessibility to telecommunications between the developed and developing world and, within the developing world, between urban and rural areas. While there are now almost 50 lines per 100 people in high income industrialized countries, there is still an average of less than one line per 100 in the poorest countries. The gaps are even greater between urban and non-urban areas. There are almost three times as many telephone lines per 100 in the largest city of lower middle income countries as in their rural areas, and more than seven times as many lines per 100 in the largest city of low-income countries as in their rural areas.

Changing telecommunications environment

An analysis of strategies for increasing access to telecommunications in developing countries must be placed in context. First, telecommunication technologies have changed dramatically in the past decade, and many recent innovations offer promising solutions for extending services at lower costs than were generally thought possible. Perhaps the most telling evidence of change is the cover of the Maitland Commission report itself, which showed two rotary dial telephones. This is not to say that digital switching did not exist by 1984, but that it was not considered necessary or perhaps even appropriate for developing regions. A second indicator is that the Commission specifically identified only telephone service, and proposed access "in due course [to] the other services telecommunications can provide." Today, many of those services could be available as soon as telecommunication service is provided.

There are many recent technological innovations that can make telecommunication services more reliable and cheaper to provide. Advances in radio technology such as cellular radio and rural radio subscriber systems offer affordable means of reaching less isolated rural customers. Cellular networks can be used for payphones and other "fixed" services as well as for mobile communications. "Wireless local loop" technologies can link subscribers to the network without the need for laying cable or stringing copper wire. Digital video can be "compressed" so that video conferencing may require as few as two 64 kilobit per second circuits. Digital audio can also be compressed so that 8 or more conversations can be carried on a 64 kbit per second channel, thus reducing transmission costs.

Voice mail systems can do much more than replace analogue answering machines. TeleBahia in north-eastern Brazil is using voice messaging technology to offer "virtual telephone service" to people who are still without individual telephone service. They can rent a voice mail box for a monthly fee. Callers can leave messages in their mail boxes, which the subscribers can retrieve from a pay phone.

Development organizations seeking cheap ways to communicate with field projects are using single satellite low earth orbiting (LEO) systems for electronic messaging. For example, SatelLife, a non-profit association of physicians based in Boston, operates "Health Net," using a micro-satellite to provide store-and-forward data communication to small terminals in developing countries.

Changing policy environment

In addition to technological change, the policy environment is also changing dramatically. The first strategy for creating incentives to improve efficiency and innovation in the telecommunication sector is to create an autonomous organization operating on business principles. This is often seen as an intermediate step between a PTT structure and some form of privatization. Most developing countries have taken this step, which is advocated by the World Bank and other funding agencies.

Privatization models range from minor investments by private companies, to joint ventures between private carriers and governments, to full privatization without any government stake or with a small government "golden share." Most countries began with a national monopoly model that is being eroded. Most maintain some level of monopoly, for example in the local loop, but alternative providers using wireless and fibre are also beginning to challenge the assumption of natural monopoly in the local loop. An intermediate step between national monopoly and competition is a policy of open entry for unserved areas. For example, the United States, Finland, Hungary an Poland have small companies or cooperatives that were formed to provide services in areas ignored by the national monopoly carrier. Competition can range from terminal equipment (now commonly competitive in most countries, including developing countries), to new services such as cellular telephony, to value-added services such as packet data networks, to full competition in the network.

Implications for planning

Changing developing economies are likely to result in new and changing demands for telecommunication services, while the introduction of new technologies is changing the economic viability of rural telecommunications.

While basic voice communication is still the first priority, many users now have requirements for data communication as well, particularly facsimile and relatively low speed data communication. Demand for Internet access is also growing enormously for universities, libraries and schools, as well as for government and business applications and private use. Thus transmission channels must be reliable enough to handle data as well as voice traffic.

The availability of relatively low cost radio and satellite technologies for serving rural areas makes it possible to reach even the most remote locations, and to base priorities for service on need rather than proximity to the terrestrial network. The combination of increased demand and lower cost technologies makes rural areas more attractive for investment. As a result, other institutional structures besides public sector monopolies may also be suitable for rural service provision.

Before taking major steps to encourage investment or restructure the telecommunication sector, planners should set national telecommunication goals. Nations in general seek to improve educational standards, to provide health care for all, to create jobs, to reduce disparities between haves and have-nots, both urban and rural.

The Maitland Commission paid little attention to the structure of the telecommunication sector beyond advocating that telecommunications be set up "as a separate, self-sustaining enterprise, run along business lines". At the time, many developing countries were still running telecommunications through a government department with revenues subsidizing the postal services, and often turning foreign exchange earnings over to the national treasury. Today, a majority of developing countries are running their telecommunication administrations as autonomous government-owned enterprises, and many are in the process of privatizing these operations.

5

Internet and Rural Development

There has been a rapid increase in the use of the Internet in developing countries, although this expansion is still largely an urban phenomenon. Rural communities represent the "last mile of connectivity" in both developing and developed countries with regard to access to Internet services and the telecommunication connections that help transmit those services. People in rural areas are generally unable to take advantage of the services available to their urban peers.Internet initiatives for rural development need to be approached with a degree of caution.

One cannot expect less privileged farmers and food-insecure residents of rural communities to list computers and digital telecommunication services as high-priority items for improving their lives. However, there are various intermediaries serving these populations which, together with small and medium enterprises (SMEs) in rural areas, could take advantage of these technologies to improve their work, improve communication capacity, gain efficiencies and reduce telecommunication costs. With SMEs, intermediary organizations such as extension field offices, rural NGOs, health clinics, government satellite offices and church organizations can offer communication services in numerous ways. Strategies for improving access to the

Internet and use for rural development will necessarily involve the full participation of intermediary organizations and other rural stakeholders. Today we truly live in a global village, but it is a village with privileged information "haves" and many information "have-nots". To face the unprecedented challenges brought on by the changing global economy, dynamic political contexts, environmental degradation and demographic pressures, and to make critical decisions, people at all levels of society - especially the food-insecure and the organizations that serve and represent them - must be able to access critical information and to communicate. Improved communication and information access are directly related to social and economic development. The Internet is a multipurpose tool, a medium of communication and perhaps the most flexible medium currently available. It has the potential to be integrated within a wide variety of efforts that have objectives such as local participation, training, education, research, technical support and institutional strengthening. Thus, endeavours that might find a role for Internet applications could range from training to the development of criteria and indicators for sustainable agriculture.

The Internet today is a people's network. Anyone with basic computer equipment and a telephone line can connect to it, communicate through it, host information on it and look through or browse it. Unlike many other media such as television and radio, every user of the medium can be an information producer and knowledge sharer. Communicating over the Internet costs a fraction of what it does to use traditional telephones or fax because information flows in discrete packets of digital bits that are able to share telecommunication lines with hundreds of other packets. Where a traditional transatlantic telephone call will tie up a single telephone line for only two people, an e-mail message can travel along a telephone line with hundreds and even thousands of other messages. A fact that is well known to veteran Internet users is that the Internet has the power to cut across social and geographic distance and help people find new ways of facilitating the flow of information and knowledge.

Agricultural Development

With regard to Internet use in support of rural and agricultural development, applications fall into five main areas: economic development for agricultural producers, community development, research/education, SME development and media networks.

Rural communities and small-scale agricultural producers are deeply affected by global economic, environmental and political forces. The idea that communities of small-scale agricultural producers are isolated and living in closed, self-sufficient societies is a myth. In fact, with the appropriate knowledge, small-scale producers can even have a competitive edge over larger operations. When knowledge is harnessed by strong organizations of small producers, strategic planning can be used to provide members with lower-cost inputs, better storage facilities, improved transportation links and collective negotiations with buyers. The Internet is one tool that can enhance this flow of information. It is an inexpensive way to communicate and access global information. Local Internet services can be easily managed by well-organized local user groups and farmers' organizations. Information and analyses can be tailored to local, regional and national knowledge and communication needs and realities. When combined with national and global market information systems, and with the ability to communicate quickly with potential buyers and brokers, local Internet systems become valuable strategic planning and decision-making tools.

Community information centres and farmers' organizations can also gather information from the Internet and disseminate it via local radio stations, newspapers and other local information-sharing networks and tools. For example, daily market prices and agricultural news can be posted at cooperatives, local stores, transportation hubs, agricultural supply outlets and social gathering points. Simple newsletters can be developed using Internet information and distributed to members of farmers' organizations. When integrated with other media tools, the Internet can be a powerful information resource and research tool.

Internet services are also valuable when placed at the service of rural development-oriented organizations which act as local communication conduits or intermediaries. Along with providing improved market knowledge, they can also:

— develop locally appropriate applications and creative services;

— provide knowledge about successful development strategies;

— enable efficient regional, national and global organizational efforts .

— improve access to a huge variety of information, training, research and educational resources (including distance education services) which are typically unavailable in rural and remote areas because of the costs associated with printed materials and books;

— enable rural young people to learn about computers and to have access to the technologies and information available to their urban peers;

— provide access to critical technical information for rural professionals such as physicians, health care workers, technicians and engineers, thereby providing further encouragement for these professionals to continue practising in rural and remote communities;

— be used as marketing tools to promote rural tourism and market the products of small secondary industries and home-based businesses;

— enable local NGOs to gain a global presence and make better contact with potential donors and supporters through the on-line publication of resources and information and through the use of electronic mail; and

— sensitize urban policy-makers to the realities and needs of rural populations.

Internet use among intermediary organizations and leaders involved in participatory research can provide a cost-effective method for documenting and sharing lessons learned and research results. Internet use also has the potential to strengthen linkages between and among farmers' organizations, extension workers, researchers and policy-makers. The cost of accessing printed academic materials within developing countries is usually so high that students and faculty members have great difficulty acquiring books and journals. Furthermore, the time required to obtain printed materials from overseas can be long enough to render some information outdated by the time it arrives. Via the Internet, any information published on-line can be accessed almost instantly and at a fraction of the cost of obtaining printed materials. Archival lists of resources can be easily reviewed and assessed in remote locations. With the assistance of Internet tools, these partnerships can be further strengthened and Internet learning resources can be cooperatively developed across oceans to be utilized by participants in developing nations. Overall, the Internet holds significant potential to enhance learning and research relationships among researchers, academics and students wherever they may be located. The list of potential applications is infinite and thousands of informal linkages of this sort take place every day in Internet discussion groups.

News Media Networks

The news media in developing countries have also been at the forefront of developing Internet applications. In addition to the latter news and information applications, organizations such as Inter Press Service (IPS) Third World News Agency use the Internet to source news stories from local writers in developing countries and share those stories with international wire services such as Associated Press. IPS is also able to provide Internet feeds that enable African news media to have access to African news from around the continent. his is particularly relevant to rural radio stations and other rural newspaper and newsletter producers that would otherwise be unable to obtain the same news from other sources. IPS can also provide an outlet for rural news writers to share their stories regionally, nationally and globally. Similar Internet strategies for rural radio networks, which might also incorporate digital audio transmissions, may well emerge in the near future.The Internet is not a panacea for rural development, but it does bring new information resources and can open new communication channels for rural communities.

It offers a means for bridging the gaps between development professionals and rural people by initiating interaction and dialogue, new alliances, interpersonal networks and cross-sectoral links between organizations. It can create mechanisms that enable the bottom-up articulation and sharing of local knowledge. Benefits include increased efficiency in the use of development resources, less duplication of activities, reduced communication costs and global access to information and human resources.

The Internet may help in meeting peoples' information and communication objectives in order to attain their development goals and objectives, but it must be integrated within human contexts and seen as a "communication process tool", not simply a static "information technology" or unit-directional broadcast medium. Otherwise, Internet tools will be relegated to the junk heaps of inappropriate development technologies or dismissed because of previous failures to make the medium locally relevant and useful. Of course, the Internet is not the only communications tool that may be used; radio and television may have equal or even greater potential, at least for the moment. We must avoid contributing to the gap between the information haves and the information have-nots that can emerge when we create Internet applications to serve only privileged researchers and bureaucrats. In particular, we must strive to find ways to bring knowledge producers, such as researchers and policy-makers, closer to the other less recognized knowledge producers: the people who are the ultimate beneficiaries of their development programmes.

Early Internet users in developing countries have proved that they can develop excellent local services and locally appropriate knowledge resources. However, without support from development agencies, there is a risk that such efforts will never meet the needs of people in rural communities.

Adopting a proactive strategy and acting to bring the Internet to rural and agricultural communities in developing countries will help enable rural people to face the unprecedented challenges brought on by the changing global economy, political changes, environmental degradation and demographic pressures. To deal with these challenges and to make critical decisions, people at all levels of society, and especially the food-insecure and the organizations that serve and represent them, must be able to access critical information and communicate.

The time to act in support of Internet knowledge and communication systems in developing countries is now. Today we truly live in a global village, but it is a village with privileged "information haves" and many "information have-nots". With the new technologies available to us, we have an opportunity to change this.

Rural Connectivity: An Exploration of Issues

Participatory approaches

Electronic communication networks (ECNs) can be used to promote participatory exchange of information, knowledge and experiences at the grass roots level. ECN is a new medium of communication, and its casting and content need to be thought through. Participatory approaches can help in ECN design and use by all involved. Before looking at the details of why and how there could be benefits, it is important for us to understand what we mean by "participatory approaches". There are many forms of participation, but the bottom line is that communities participate genuinely if they will derive benefits aimed at satisfying their real felt needs as they define them themselves. These benefits need not solely be material benefits - material benefits only make sense when they satisfy communities' fundamental needs such as subsistence, identity, freedom, protection, affection, understanding, participation, creation and leisure.

If participation is a basic need, it is worth looking at the typology of different types of participation so as to put the type of participation that empowers communities in the context of other non-genuine forms of participation.

Structurally, villagers should have an understanding of the systems involved. They need to understand the system of networking they are involved in. This is important if they are to be empowered to get maximum benefit out of the system. Like designing any communication programme, and the communication media and activities that go with it, designing an ECN has several challenges if it is done in a participatory manner:

— how to design the system properly through research of the needs of key interaction groups including rural groups, the community, change agents, or facilitators if involved; and

— how to design the system properly through a participatory design process.

Such assessment would focus on issues such as:

— segmentation of interaction groups by such factors as gender, age groups, occupation, wealth, etc.;

— content identification;

— subjects and purpose, for example, for awareness, entertainment or training;

— packaging of the interface and the content;

— using visuals or audio-visuals to assist overcoming gaps of literacy; and

— activities that encourage responses.

Some ECN materials may need to be tailored to specific audiences, but this does not preclude connection to the Internet although it focuses on immediate needs for purposes of encouraging participation and developmental objectives. A major issue is how the system will be designed to bridge the first mile with participatory approaches that use other media and channels to encourage people's inputting and receiving relevant information, knowledge and experiences to and from the network, even though they do not have direct access to the computer.

Information sharing and communication

Through participatory rural communication appraisal, establish how 'a' wants communication coming from 'b', 'c', 'd', or 'e', to be packaged when it is received and the type of information wanted from each different point. The reverse is equally true; that is, each point can establish how 'a' can send particular types of information they need in terms of packaging.

Electronic communication networking could easily supercharge the speed of everything from cash flow to customer services in a community. The network in this case is not only a means of facilitating business but the business itself. Since important activities cannot be entrusted to one person, the community will need to be organized/ reorganized to deal with the new changes in communication. Changes in communication of this nature bring extreme changes like free-flowing information, and the community needs to be organised for this. Information is power, and investing it in few hands could disempower the other villagers. This can be overcome by group rather than individual training.

Village activities are usually conducted under a big tree or in a big grass thatched enclosure with the people sitting together, circular fashion that is intimate. Information received (e.g., for training, marketing, inputs, prices, etc.) could be enlarged from a PC monitor to an overhead projector screen and the villagers could together or in groups discuss and strategize on what action to take next. As soon as they make their decision they could respond via the same medium. Juxtaposed to this is the possibility of the extension worker, the facilitator at village level, being an information worker too. This means people can still meet under the big tree or big grass thatched hut and discuss information they have received and plan together sending back replies. However, the information worker will also play the role of decoding a lot of information, which could be difficult to comprehend or respond to. Although emphasis is placed on group activity, we should not make it seem a must. Whereas in nascent community organizations group approaches are strong, in emergent and mature community organization decisions taken collectively are more and more delegated to individuals to implement or critique.

If people cannot read and write it is not the end of the world. Programmes can be designed so that people understand interaction in the written word with regards to specific functions. This has been known to work very well with teaching bookkeeping to village groups involved in small-scale enterprises.

Villagers are not concerned about into food security only. A resource such as electronic communication network would be under-utilised if left for one function only. The people may like such a resource to be linked to development of other things like a library, information on opportunities for school leavers and entertainment. Participatory approaches could also establish different preferred information and communication needs.

The systems, the technology itself and the atmosphere should be sensitive to the needs of women, men, children, adults and old people. If conflicts arise in use or content or type of technology, villagers would need to be familiar with conflict mediation and resolution.

Impacts of the Internet on Unconnected Rural Areas

The impacts of non-governmental organizations with Internet connectivity on rural communities represents an attempt to address the shortcomings of previous ICT evaluations. It is not meant to be a definitive study of how to examine rural communities' information sharing with NGOs possessing Internet connectivity, but it does propose a framework from which to build upon, improve, and make as relevant as possible an understanding of the benefits and impacts of the Internet for those who lack connectivity in rural areas of developing countries. Only through application in the field can such frameworks be tested, assessed, and improved upon. It is hoped that this framework represents a fresh approach to understanding the complex issues and networks involved in information sharing and ICT use.

Much of the literature on the use of information and communication technologies (ICT) concerns the potential that such investments offer for the developing world. Yet despite the rhetoric of how ICT can bridge the gap between the information haves and the have-nots, there is little research available that demonstrates that the use of ICT are in fact able to bridge that gap. Moreover, the focus of ICT research is currently fixated on the institutional level, which is composed of Internet service providers (ISPs), policy makers and governments. While the value of such research is not challenged here, the fact remains that very little investigation has been conducted concerning the impacts of ICT on those who have the most to gain through the expansion of ICT in the developing world: the rural stakeholder communities.

The benefits of expanding ICT to major urban cities has been well-documented, and the results of such urban investment can be seen in both the expansion of ISPs and the increasing connectivity throughout the cities of the developing world. Furthermore, the economics involved in development agencies' and corporations' willingness to expand Internet connectivity into rural areas in both Northern and Southern hemispheres has proven to be a major stumbling block. In fact, rather than expansion being based upon the desire to meet the communication needs of rural communities, rural ICT expansion is primarily based on the degree to which it will be a profitable and worthwhile venture for the communication companies involved.

The exclusion of rural communities and stakeholders from ICT expansion occurs in spite of the benefits that ICT is intended to bring to the isolated areas of the world. Even with the inclusion of the two questions relating to local stakeholders' acceptance, support, and ability to assume ownership of ICT, the CIDA report offers vague, insufficient analysis of the rural impacts of ICT. This is evidenced in the presentation of a case study of a Peruvian rural telephone expansion project; the report states that the project's immediate impact is an increase in telecommunications access for 200 000 people. Beyond this statistic, however, the report was unable to identify any of the direct and indirect impacts of this project at the community level.

There is a need to refocus ICT research so that the communication processes occurring with the use of the Internet are examined, rather than the infrastructural components themselves. Through learning how communities without Internet connectivity are able to benefit from organizations that have connectivity, and through learning how the two entities can work together to ensure that information is received, shared, and put to good use, those in development can move towards guaranteeing that stakeholders' needs are being met, and that adequate support is provided to those who need it most. If the benefits of the Internet are not made available to the rural peoples who can benefit from it the most, "then we are failing to fully leverage the large infrastructure investments involved, and we are failing to assist people in making appropriate decisions based on such valuable information".

The concept of participatory development communication is central to examining the use of the Internet as it relates to rural community stakeholders. Its basic tenet is that, "the communication process is more important than the production of media products". Participatory communication for development is a process that emphasizes a two-way communication process based on sharing ideas and information in order to improve the quality of life of the stakeholder communities. Unlike traditional com-munication methods of disseminating and transmitting information, development for communication "is about aiding different types of actors interested in understanding needs and assessing opportunities jointly; it is about providing them with the methods and media to reach common meaning, and about enabling them to negotiate with other actors with contrasting perceptions and interests".

The Internet is the latest in a long line of communication tools that enable a community to receive information and assistance from outside organizations. Unlike technologies such as radio, newspaper, and video, however, the Internet, "is the first media tool that allows every user to be a sender, receiver, narrowcaster and broadcaster". The tremendous opportunities that such technology can offer to rural stakeholder communities must not be missed. The challenge, however, is ensuring that the Internet is utilized for two-way communication processes such as communicating local knowledge and perceptions.

Towards a New Evaluation Approach

Current evaluations tend to ignore those rural stakeholders who are without connectivity. The need exists for an evaluation approach that will specifically examine the impacts of ICT on development at a grassroots level. Michel Menou writes of the importance of understanding the grassroots' impacts from the Internet when he states that "lower level data are needed to interpret higher trends". He goes further in suggesting the importance of focusing on this segment of the population when discussing the issue of equality of access to information.

Such access, "must also be considered in relation to its effectiveness for the worst-off segments of the population, such as handicapped people or geographically scattered rural populations. The time to focus on the processes that accompany technological tools such as the Internet is now. Without understanding how ICT such as the Internet are impacting those at the grassroots level, we risk remaining unaware of the effectiveness of technological investments that occur at the institutional level.

6

Internet and Agricultural Development

The Internet is not a panacea for rural and agricultural development, but it does bring new information resources and can open up new communication channels for rural communities and agricultural organizations. It offers a means for bridging the gaps between development professionals, rural people and agricultural producers through the initiation of interaction and dialogue. It can foster new alliances and interpersonal networks together with lateral and cross-sector links between organizations.

Most importantly, it can support mechanisms that enable the bottom-up articulation and sharing of information on needs and local knowledge. Primary benefits include increased efficiency in the use of development resources, less duplication of activities, reduced communication costs and global access to information and human resources. None of these benefits are guaranteed by the technology of the Internet. Instead, they are realized when people work together to make the most of a decentralized and accessible communication tool. There has been a rapid increase in the use of the Internet in developing countries. With regard to rural and agricultural development and the Internet, organizations that support the betterment of rural populations and improvements in agriculture have important roles to play. For example, the Food and Agriculture Organization of the United Nations, is playing an important role in assisting the establishment and growth of Internet services for rural communities and for agricultural development. In partnership with local stakeholders and other development agencies, organizations like FAO can help rural communities and agricultural organizations realize the benefits of improved communication and access to information.

Enormous benefits await rural communities and agricultural organizations when communication improves between the non-governmental organizations, government services, private sector entities and educational institutes that support rural and agricultural development. By sharing information about their activities in the fields of agriculture, rural development, forestry, fisheries, health, nutrition, and education, these agencies can better serve rural people and farmers. They can make use of "lessons learned," determine and use "best practices," and coordinate information about particular regions or successful development approaches. At the same time, rural communities and agricultural organizations can benefit equally from improved vertical channels of communication that enable rural stakeholders and farmers to communicate with decision-makers and others concerned with development.

An integrated approach to the expansion of Internet services will promote the necessary (but often neglected) horizontal communication between agencies linked to rural and agricultural development. At the same time, an integrated approach will provide the tools to enable rural people and farmers to enter directly into new vertical communication relationships with external agencies. Improving horizontal communication can improve the quality and relevance of information resources and and physical resources available to rural people. Improving vertical communication between rural people, farmers and decision-makers can improve the quality of decisions that affect rural communities and agricultural organizations.

An integrated approach provides for vertical communication by establishing rural Internet access sites, and by enhancing horizontal communication between such entities as agricultural colleges, agricultural input and equipment suppliers, government extension services, rural development organizations, health care agencies, and agricultural research and documentation centres. Improved horizontal communication can also include existing media services that serve rural stakeholders. For example, throughout the developing world, rural radio and, increasingly, television broadcast services, are important information delivery mechanisms. Their services improve significantly through the exchange of information and news by way of the Internet. African news items are commonly circulated among African news agencies via the Internet.

Rural African radio stations are able to take advantage of Internet services to provide extension and rural development information from qualified research sources from around the world. Internet services, in conjunction with existing and more widely used communication media such as rural radio, will enable the broadest enhancement of information and communication resources for rural people. For example, national or regional agricultural market information systems or extension information systems hosted on the Internet can be excellent information sources for the staff of rural radio stations throughout a region or nation.

Using information on current market prices broadcast by rural radio stations, farmers can negotiate better prices from local buyers. Improved horizontal communication and improved information resources can improve the quality of the decisions and interventions that impact upon rural people. At the same time, these improvements can enhance rural peoples' direct participation in development. Establishing rural Internet access sites and facilities in concert with efforts to enhance horizontal communication networks among the agencies involved in rural and agricultural development is the essence of the integrated approach highlighted.

Sustainability and Success

Current evidence suggests that to achieve sustainability and success, Internet projects for rural and agricultural development must begin with the real needs of the local community of users. This requires an approach that catalyzes local participation, supports information and communication needs assessments, creates awareness of potential Internet uses, helps build communities of users, and facilitates locally managed, self-supporting communication and information networks. It also requires attention to capacity building and institutional strengthening for the intermediary agencies that serve rural populations so that they can make the most appropriate and creative use of Internet tools.

At the policy level, the success of Internet projects in development requires dialogue with national telecommunication agencies to help transform and liberalize the monopolistic telecommunication service environments common in developing countries. Monopolistic services tend to stifle the technological innovation, infrastructure investment and price improvements that often come with competition. Many analysts indicate that where telecommunication reforms have occurred, telecommunication services have "expanded and improved at a faster pace, productivity has increased, new services have become available, and in some cases, international capital markets have been tapped effectively.

A communication for development methodology typically begins with partnerships with local people and organizations to assist them in developing local communication processes by using tools such as community radio and small format video. At the same time, these initiatives work in concert with projects to create national agricultural information and communication networks that strengthen information sharing both horizontally and vertically. Such integrated approaches are achieving important economic and social benefits for rural users, while enabling national agencies to realize significant interorganizational efficiencies.

Communication for development methodologies deserve wider understanding. They are linked to participatory development methodologies and resemble basic computer systems analysis approaches which should start with the needs of computer users. Communication for development methodologies do, however, provide development planners with a conceptual approach that puts rural people, rural organizations farmers and agricultural organizations in positions where they can help direct communication and information network development. Communication for development methodologies can be important factors in achieving sustainable development:

An integrated rural Internet development approach also requires leadership among individuals who can put aside considerations of institutional competition. Such leaders must demonstrate, through action, their belief in the value of information sharing over information hoarding, and their dedication to rural and agricultural development. Without enthusiastic champions, most Internet projects will fail. It is not enough for development planners to build wonderful network systems and provide people with computers and modems. Potential users must identify with a vision for beneficial applications, and they are most likely to respond to the visions of enthusiastic peers and colleagues. This vast project was initially led by only three young civil servants with a small budget and the support of a handful of high level government champions. In its early stages the project met with a great deal of resistance across many ministries. Despite resistance, the project staff worked diligently to identify and empower institutional champions, most of whom were located at relatively low levels within the Government.

Within two years, almost every Government ministry had at least one champion working to place useful information on the Internet and strengthen links between ministries and with the public. As the public became more adept at accessing available Government information, they began to demand more resources, while often providing vocal praise for the initiatives underway. Before long, a momentum had developed that could no longer be resisted by reluctant bureaucrats, and eventually the provision of government information on the Internet became a matter of public policy. Parallel federal and provincial government efforts to strengthen community, private sector and educational access to the Internet helped push further demands for government information, along with mechanisms for engaging the government in new forms of electronic dialogue.

Rural communities around the world tend to be under serviced in their access to the various technologies, Internet services and telecommunication connections that help transmit those services. In Canada, poor Internet access relates directly to a poor rural telecommunication infrastructure. This situation is the result of antiquated telephone lines in many rural areas combined with a general policy myopia about the needs and desires of rural people. Several developing countries have better rural telecommunication systems than many parts of rural Canada.

This situation is changing quickly, and the Internet is the catalyst. Rural peoples' desires to use the Internet are resulting in unprecedented and vocal demands for rural telecommunication improvements. In Canada, strong rural Internet champions are emerging from agricultural producer organizations rural economic development agencies, health care groups and educational bodies. Their advocacy efforts are quickly leading to change and to government and private sector support for rural telecommunication enhancement and Internet support services. In the last eighteen months, over 50 rural and agricultural producer organizations in the province of Ontario alone have joined the Internet community by establishing electronic information resources.

The Internet has sparked an unprecedented interest in telecommunication infrastructure among people who previously had little interest in telephone wires. A decade ago telephone systems could only be expected to carry voice conversations between two people. Now they are expected to move vast libraries of information, photographs, music and even video while enabling dozens of people to communicate with one another at the same time. Where once we could tolerate static and interference during a telephone call over poor rural telephone lines, we tend to become quickly frustrated by the very same lines when they are responsible for limiting our access to information and multiple communication channels.

The demand for telecommunication improvement tends to be most acute among those who are most marginalized from information resources and communication services: rural people, rural organizations and farmers' groups. People who once had very little interest in telecommunication infrastructure are now learning what they need to know to advocate for the communication and information tools they desire. In some cases, rural people and farmers take it upon themselves to create their "homegrown" services when established telecommunication bodies do not meet the demand. Evidence of this can be found throughout the developing world. Examples include the entrepreneurial farmers in Zambia who are working to create a rural telecommunication infrastructure based on new digital wireless and fiber optic technologies, and farmers in northern Mexico who have created an Internet service to enable producer organizations to better communicate and access market information.

Integrated Rural and Agricultural Development

Investments in development require vision. Development initiatives that involve technology will sometimes lose sight of the human dimensions of development. The goal of an integrated approach to improving Internet services for rural and agricultural development is to enable rural people to increase the community resources they require to improve their lives. Communication networks that enable information to flow to and from rural communities and agricultural organizations as well as between and among the many intermediary organizations that touch rural communities and farmers directly or indirectly, will strengthen community resources. This requires a vision of all the stakeholders involved in rural and agricultural development communicating with one another, with rural organizations and people having access to the same communication tools and information resources as their urban peers.

The Internet suits this vision well. The Internet is a medium of communication, and is perhaps the most flexible medium currently available. It has the potential for integration within a wide variety of projects that have objectives such as local participation, training, education, research (especially participatory research), technical support and institutional strengthening. In short, it is a tool that can be of value to integrated rural and agricultural development. Whenever a project involves people who need to communicate and share information across geography, across social groupings, between organizations and throughout production systems, there is a need to create flexible systems of communication and information sharing. Thus, projects that might find a role for Internet applications could range from apiculture training to community forestry to veterinary medicine.

The Internet is a multipurpose tool that, in its essence, enables people to learn from one another and work together. The results of Internet projects are not technical, but human and social. The Internet is essentially a tool for enhancing human relationships. Projects need to be driven, not by technical concerns, but by human knowledge, communication, and social relationship concerns. Thus, the intended results of an Internet project ought to relate directly to improvements in social relationships, improvements in knowledge sharing and knowledge access, and enhancement of communication among people and organizations. Such project results can happen through efforts to increase rural community resources and agricultural resources to achieve project outputs (depending upon local circumstances) such as:

— locally developed learning tools, learning games, learning networks;

— interactive and collaborative extension information networks among farmer organizations government extension services, rural media, research bodies and educational institutions;

— rural "folk schools" and "farmer field schools" similar to those created by rural radio, and non-formal education initiatives such as farm radio forums and radio listening groups;

— market information networks (regional, national, local);

— distance learning programmes and networks;

— participatory research and action networks;

— interactive and collaborative "expert systems" and decision-support networks;

— early warning system information dissemination and data gathering networks;

— shared curriculum databases and curriculum development networks; research sharing and information dissemination systems;

— training tools;

— small and medium enterprise development networks and marketing mechanisms;

— rural media networks (e.g. rural radio, newsletters, etc.);

— agro-ecosystem health networks;

— indigenous knowledge networks;

— disease and pest monitoring action networks (plant and animal); water management information networks;

— agricultural product and service trading networks (regional, national, local).

Improving rural community information and communication resources must also link to efforts to improve the capacity of rural organizations and rural people to make the most effective, and sustainable, use of those resources. Internet initiatives for rural and agricultural development need to be approached with a degree of caution. Different regions, organizations and communities will have different application, capacity building and technical needs. In some areas it is possible to have farmers and rural residents as direct Internet users (e.g. Chile, Mexico). In other areas, the challenge will be to help build the capacity of intermediary organizations (such as extension field offices, NGOs, rural schools, libraries, health clinics, government satellite offices, and church organizations or assist in the establishment and promotion of community information centres linked to the Internet. In all cases, it will be important to link Internet activities with existing media and local communication methods and patterns.

Every initiative is likely to have its own unique characteristics as a result of the unique characteristics of the local people involved and their social, cultural and economic backgrounds. Special attention also needs to be given to women's involvement in these initiatives. Overall, there are more male Internet users than female Internet users. North American surveys place the ratio in that region of the world at between three and four to one, male to female Internet users. This situation seems to be improving over time. However, special efforts must be made to insure that women have a chance for early participation in new Internet initiatives for rural and agricultural development. Concern for gender equity is one reason for this recommendation. Another is evidence which suggests that women can play a role in ensuring that community oriented Internet services remain focused on community needs and do not get carried away by technological gimmickry.

Communication Development Approach

FAO's twenty-five year experience with a communication for development approach to rural and agricultural communication, using media such as rural radio, small format video (participatory video), photography and print, is now being applied to the Internet in three small scale initiatives. This simple and common-sense strategy of involving people in assessments of their knowledge and communication needs is the cornerstone of communication for development methodologies. Much of FAO's success with communication for development approaches has involved the use of a medium that many development planners first dismissed as too "high-tech" and as being inappropriate technology. This medium is small format video (consumer grade video cameras and portable television monitors). Facilitators use small format video to enable rural residents to articulate their ideas, aspirations, needs and solutions.

Using video, people can speak directly to distant decision makers and researchers, gain access to knowledge presented in audiovisual form by experts (often other farmers), and share their experiences with one another across distances. In participatory video work, the communication process is more important than the production of a video. This aspect of the process is frequently misunderstood by observers of communication for development projects. It is not important for participants to become communication professionals: the goal is to provide media that are flexible enough to allow people to articulate and share their ideas.

Integrated into development planning activities, such a communication for development approach enables farmers and rural people to actively participate in development processes. These approaches enable rural stakeholders to articulate their knowledge, organize local activities, take part in decision making and fully recognize the value of sharing their ideas. Like participatory video processes, the Internet may help people to attain their development goals, but it must be used as a communication process tool and not simply as a static "information technology." Otherwise, Internet tools will be relegated to the junk heaps of inappropriate development technologies or dismissed because of previous failures to make the medium locally relevant and useful.

If, for example, the information outputs derived from highly technical electronic information systems such as famine early warning systems or food security databases are not made available to the people whose lives are the subject of those systems, then we are failing to fully exploit the large infrastructure investments involved, and we are failing to assist people in making appropriate decisions based on such valuable information. Before we even create such tools, we ought to involve the ultimate beneficiaries in determining the value of these initiatives and discussing planning approaches.

A fact that is well known to current Internet users is that the Internet has the power to cut across social and geographic distance and help people find new ways of facilitating the flow of information and knowledge. In many ways the Internet has always been a development communication tool. Within bureaucratic organizations it has a way of levering hierarchies, facilitating new communication patterns, and helping enable activities that might not otherwise occur. This factor makes it an especially attractive medium within communication for development efforts. The key to achieving similar results in new Internet and development projects is to begin with a grassroots, beneficiary-inclusive communication for development approach during the planning process.

Internet and Development Initiatives

The range of locally initiated Internet services in developing countries is remarkable. Many of these services have emerged with little or no external support, and many have become viable commercial services or not-for-profit services operated by NGOs. A large number of these Internet services have been around for almost a decade, coming into existence years before most donor agencies recognized any potential in the Internet as a development tool. Today, however, many international development agencies and international NGOs are finding ways to assist in the development and strengthening of local Internet services, infrastructure and information providers.

Despite the wide range of organizations supporting Internet services and applications in developing countries, obtaining accurate and up-to-date information on these activities is difficult. Donor agencies and project staff are not communicating about their initiatives very well. Despite the obvious potential of the Internet for sharing information on Internet projects, there is no single source that enables interested parties to quickly access information on specific projects, country activities and donor agency strategies and plans. As a result, the lessons being learned are being lost. Leaders in the donor agency community must remedy this problem soon to ensure that lessons learned are shared and that interested parties can quickly and easily identify opportunities for collaboration and for using Internet services and applications in developing countries.

The Internet was conceived in 1963 by Larry Roberts while he was working for the Advanced Research Projects Agency (ARPA) with funding from the United States Department of Defence. The fact that, at its essence, the Internet is a human relationship enhancement tool is reflected in its history, and the very human relationships of its early developers. ARPAnet, as it was called in the beginning, emerged as a communication tool in the late 1960s for a handful of Defence workers and contractors. It was designed as a fundamentally *decentralized* network in order to be a fail-safe communication system.

Computers could send packets of information from one computer to another, across the United States, and those packets could travel through a variety of different routes to reach their destination. If one or several routes were destroyed or malfunctioning, the packets would find alternative routes and eventually reach their destinations. The wife of one of the ARPAnet engineers was hearing impaired. To communicate with her while he was at the office and she was at home, the engineer used a telephone attachment that was then commonly used in the United States. A telephone text messaging device (TTY) enabled him and his wife to converse through text messages sent through the telephone system. This relationship enhancing tool influenced the engineer to incorporate text messaging between people (not just between computers) as a feature of ARPAnet. This feature became known as electronic mail or e-mail, and now millions of e-mail messages cries-cross the globe every day. As a result of one person's positive experience with a similar relationship enhancing tool, what was initially a tool for computers to talk to computers became a tool for enhancing relationships.

ARPAnet grew during the late 1960s and throughout the 1970s because new "nodes" and routes were added to reach university researchers. As a wider community of faculty members and students outside the Department of Defence began to use the tool, electronic mail quickly gained popularity across university and college campuses in North America. Because it was a decentralized network, there was little way to control its popular expansion, and it soon transcended its Department of Defence mentors. The Internet today is a peoples' network. Anyone with basic computer equipment and a phone line can connect to it, communicate through it, host information on it, and look through it.

Unlike many other media, such as television and radio, every user of the medium can be an information producer and knowledge sharer. No one knows for sure how many people are using the Internet today, but estimates range from 50 to 100 million people, and it is growing fast. In countries such as Thailand, Internet use is growing at a current rate of close to 1 000 percent per year. The Internet is essentially millions of people connected together via millions of computers that are connected together.

There are at least five million information-containing computers serving information to the millions and millions of Internet users. Each of those five million computers may contain thousands, or hundreds of thousands of pages of information. If current trends continue, there will be over 100 million computers connected to the Internet by the year 2000. Any one of those computers linked to the Internet might support one individual or thousands of individuals, together with the wealth of information they can contribute to the Internet. There are two powerful tools that form the basis of the Internet. The earliest on the scene, and still the most popular, is e-mail. Using a simple address to guide them, e-mail messages jump from computer to computer, rapidly finding their way to their recipients.

The more recent tool, and the one that has catapulted the Internet into popular culture, is the World Wide Web. The World Wide Web is the part of the Internet where we are witnessing the emergence of a vast global library of information. Electronic publishing of information on the World Wide Web is much less expensive than print publication. It is also very easy to become a provider of information on the World Wide Web and have people use your information almost instantaneously from virtually any location in the world. As a result, the World Wide Web is propagated with information on every subject imaginable.

In fact, an Internet user who wants to publish a work can do so for little or no money and make that work available around the globe. The World Wide Web is in its infancy, having only been developed in 1994, yet only three years after its birth it is one of the most popular information sharing tools in the world. Use of the World Wide Web is growing at a rate of 25 percent per month and it is estimated that some 100 to 400 new information sites are established on the World Wide Web each week. Prior to the World Wide Web, Internet users were limited to e-mail communication and cumbersome methods for retrieving files of information from other computers.

The World Wide Web changed that quite dramatically. Now we can retrieve information, documents, and a wide variety of audiovisual material simply by pointing and clicking. We do not even have to know the location of the computer from which we retrieve information. We just click on a highlighted word, or a picture, and within moments a document is transported to the screen in front of us. Some argue that the Internet's World Wide Web is humanity's second major communication revolution, the first being the Gutenburg Press in 1439.

Compared to the costs of using telephones or faxes, communicating and sharing information using e-mail or the World Wide Web can be hundreds of times less expensive. Because information flows through the Internet in discrete packets of digital bits, those packets are able to share telecommunication lines with hundreds of other packets. Where a traditional transatlantic telephone call will tie up a single phone line for only two people, an e-mail message can travel along a phone line with hundreds and even thousands of other messages. Some creative computer software developers have even made use of this feature of the Internet to create Internet telephone services that allow users to speak with other users around the globe, while completely avoiding long distance phone charges.

Elements of Successful Rural and Agricultural Internet Communication

Twelve common elements can be identified among successful rural and agricultural Internet communication and information systems:

1. Preliminary participatory communication and information needs assessments with intended users.
2. Awareness building campaigns designed to sensitize decision makers to the possible uses of Internet services.
3. Executing agency commitment to participatory rural and agricultural development.
4. Local "champions" identified and supported.
5. Open participation of user community in design, implementation and management of communication and information services.
6. Institutional and user commitment to manage and sustain Internet services.
7. Involvement of the full community of users, including women and youth.
8. Ongoing provision for technical training, user support and outreach within the user community.
9. Combination of centralized and decentralized information production, analysis and distribution.
10. Ongoing provision for technical support and system maintenance/ upgrading.
11. User community financial commitment in communication and information systems (e.g. ownership of hardware, user fees, salaries, infrastructure, etc.).

12. Social service orientation of local private sector or not-for-profit (university or NGO) Internet service providers.

Local private sector or not-for-profit Internet service providers tend to be able to operate efficiently and profitably while providing customers with reasonable service prices. They are able to quickly troubleshoot and solve service problems, they can access capital through investment and credit (not as easily obtained with government-focused or donor agency services), and they are able to offer strong local user support, customer troubleshooting (often with house calls), and local training. Because they are dependent upon customer revenue for profitability, they are likely to respond quickly to customer needs and demands. Government operated ISPs tend to be less able to meet customer needs and are often less responsive because they have other sources of support than customer fees. Local private sector and not-for-profit ISPs also contribute to the local economy and stimulate local interest in telecommunication through personal contacts and relationships.

In 1994, as part of FAO's Latin American communication for development effort, community animators initiated an extensive participatory communication and information needs assessment among six hundred local farmers and their organizations The results indicated that farmers strongly desired an improved communication system, and local leaders required a better management communication system for organizing activities and for agricultural and irrigation planning among 23 local organizations The farmers also wanted better methods for general communication and information sharing to assist in the planning of current and future work and activities. One strategy that they proposed was a computer-based communication system that would provide for both horizontal and vertical communication.

A communication for development expert from FAO provided initial logistical coordination and technical backstopping for the first nine months of the initiative. A computer network server was installed at the university and each farmer organization was issued an account for dial-in access to a small pool of three modems connected to the server. By June of 1996, 12 farmers' organizations were connected and using the system, several World Wide Web information services were available, and plans were being made to improve the system and involve all 23 farmers' organizations in the Rio Colorado Valley. Existing users make use of e-mail on a daily basis, and submit daily reports on irrigation quotas and planting activities to the local irrigation water authority.

The farmers are proud of their community and its history, so they decided to organize a photography contest to collect historical photographs of the region and its agricultural heritage to place on their World Wide Web homepage. They are planning to post their newsletters on the homepage as well, and hope to provide easy access to locally relevant market and weather information. Links will soon be made with the Technical Information and Communication Unit (TICU) to expand access to TICU's market information bulletin (currently distributed in Sonora by fax) by placing bulletin information on the CETYS University server for access throughout Mexico and the world (personal communication with Emilio Canton, FAO-Mexico).

These farmers' organizations have proven that Internet communication and information services are practical and beneficial when developed with full participation of users.

While the system has a long way to go in order to develop further applications and enhance user involvement with new applications, it is already attracting significant interest within the Mexican Ministry of Agriculture and other farmer organizations in Mexico. For example, Assistance and Services for Agricultural Marketing (ASERCA) is investigating the Mexicali experience in order to develop strategies for expanding farmer access to electronic information services related to marketing and the development of national and international trading links.

There are even plans for developing an electronic trading system for agricultural products and services. The development communication approach used to form the Mexicali system is the key to its initial success and its future sustainability. Using this approach has enabled the organizational leaders to fully understand the value of the system and its applications, and led to the farmers' decision to take ownership of the infrastructure and network development.

These networks provide farmer organizations with data on crops, international crop status and market timing, prices, market conditions (regional, national, international), weather, technical and training information, and information about the various organizations that support their work. The users also have full access to the Internet to find other information relevant to their lives and communities (e.g. health, social service, education, etc.), and they can use electronic mail to communicate with other farm organizations in Chile, as well as any of the millions of people using the global Internet.

The most important aspect of this initiative is its specific attention to local information needs assessments, and provision of assistance to farm organization personnel to help them develop the skills necessary to analyse and disseminate information that is locally relevant. This methodology emerged from previous development communication experiences using small format video, print media and rural radio. It is very likely the most user oriented approach to developing Internet services in the developing world, and it is focused on rural and remote agricultural communities that would normally have little opportunity to access the benefits of Internet tools.

Small information centres are located within the offices of farmer organizations and NGOs, and some of these offices are beginning to open up their Internet resources to non-agricultural community members such as youth groups and social service agencies. The network of users is currently small (five organizations and may become a model for the development of a much wider network within Chile, and, with some external assistance, throughout Latin America. Much of the information available through the Chilean network is useful to other Spanish speaking Internet users (the same is true for the Mexican initiatives discussed above).

The Mexican and Chilean experiences are unique examples of using a communication for development approach to create horizontal and vertical communication systems for small producers and rural and remote communities. Throughout the other countries visited on the author's FAO fact-finding mission, it was generally observed that access to the Internet in rural and remote areas is emerging slowly. To their credit, many organizations in Africa, including FAO and its supported projects, are developing World Wide Web based information tools that may someday be of direct benefit to small producers and rural and remote communities.

In Zambia and Zimbabwe, for example, FAO projects are busy developing Internet-based market information tools, household food security information systems, famine early warning systems and ether sophisticated tools to assist decision makers. These systems are developed primarily by researchers and policy making bodies to fulfill their own internal information needs. Thus far, links to the ultimate beneficiaries of these initiatives are weak.

In Africa, local and regional Internet service providers such as ZamNet (which also services the HealthNet project that connects rural health centres to the Internet), SangoNet, MangoNet, Enda-Dakar and Internet Africa, appear to be the only organizations with the tangible experience of providing Internet services to organizations and individuals in rural and remote areas. Their track records speak for themselves. They have managed to provide Internet services to many of the intermediary organizations that serve small producers, rural communities and agricultural organizations.

Many of the field officers of UN agencies and multilateral donor projects make use of electronic mail and Internet information services provided by these local services. The individuals who work within these Internet service providers tend to be extremely dedicated to their work and to improving Internet service in Africa. These services are "natural" examples of the horizontal and vertical communication channels essential to the integrated approach.

Future Internet development activities for rural communities and farm organizations in Africa and Latin America ought to begin with the experiences and services of existing Internet service providers and existing user groups. There is a wealth of experience, talent, creativity and local understanding available, and development agencies would be wise to utilize these resources at every opportunity.

Sustainable Rural Agricultural Development in Internet Applications

With regard to Internet use in support of rural and agricultural development, applications fall into five main areas: economic development for agricultural producers, community development, research/education, small and medium enterprise (SME) development, and media networks. Rural communities and small-scale agricultural producers are deeply affected by global economic, environmental and political forces. The idea that communities of small-scale agricultural producers are isolated and living in closed, self-sufficient societies is a myth.

Global trade relationships, such as GATT, NAFTA, and MERCOSUR, place rural communities and small-scale agricultural producers squarely in the middle of global market realities. Trade decisions in Rome or Chicago today affect campesinos in Mexico within hours. Interest rates, global commodity situations, changing trade patterns, transportation developments and tariff structures all impact upon even the smallest farm operation. Without knowledge and without the communication capabilities required to access, analyse and share the information required to create knowledge, small producers remain at the mercy of global market forces.

With knowledge, small producers can have a competitive footing with larger farm operations and corporate agriculture. Small producers often have the flexibility to quickly change crop choices, develop products for small niche markets and even market directly to the consumer or commodity broker in distant countries. Small-scale, labour intensive farming can reduce input costs and provide consumers with higher food quality, improved food safety and better food taste.

When knowledge is harnessed by strong organizations of small producers, strategic planning can be used to provide members with lower cost inputs, better storage facilities, improved transportation links and collective negotiations with buyers. Organizations of small producers want and need instant information on global market prices, negotiation techniques and strategies, analyses of product potentials in various markets, new production and marketing techniques, new transportation systems, and global trade rules. Information that can reduce the costs of transactions and improve prices received at markets (or open new markets) is highly valued. These organizations can and do act as communication conduits or intermediaries, facilitating the flow of information between local people and the rest of the world.

The global Internet is one tool that can enhance this flow of information for organizations of small producers. It is an inexpensive way to communicate and access global information. Local Internet services can be easily managed by well-organized local user groups and farmer organizations. Information and analyses can be tailored to local, regional and national knowledge and communication needs and realities. When combined with national and global market information systems, and with the ability to communicate quickly with potential buyers and brokers, local Internet systems become valuable strategic planning and decision making tools.

Local agricultural producers can benefit from the Internet without having access to computers or phone lines. Community information centre personnel can easily post market prices at places where farmers gather, can liaise with local radio stations and newspapers, and can channel information through interpersonal networks, simple newsletters and posters. Used wisely, the Internet can be part of an extended media mix for both gathering information from vertical channels and disseminating information through existing horizontal communication channels.

Applications of Community Development

Local community oriented Internet services are also valuable when placed in the service of rural and agricultural development organizations which act as local communication conduits or intermediaries. Along with providing improved market knowledge, they can also:

— develop locally appropriate applications and creative services;

— provide knowledge about successful development strategies;

— enable efficient regional, national and global organizational efforts (the use of the Internet as a global communication and organising tool in Chiapas, Mexico is an excellent example of the latter);

— provide improved access to a huge variety of information, training, research and educational resources (including distance education services) that are typically unavailable in rural and remote areas due to the costs associated with accessing printed materials and books;

- enable rural young people to learn about computers and to have access to the technologies and information available to their urban peers;
- provide access to critical technical information for rural professionals such as physicians, health care workers, technicians and engineers, thereby providing further encouragement for these professionals to continue practicing in rural and remote communities;
- be used as marketing tools to promote rural tourism and market the products of small secondary industries and home-based businesses;
- enable local NGOs to gain a global presence and make better contact with potential donors and supporters through on-line publication of resources and information, and through the use of electronic mail; and
- sensitize urban policy makers to the realities and needs of rural populations.

Research applications

Within national, regional and international research communities, there is increased attention toward "participatory research" strategies. These strategies place farmers and rural residents at the centre of the research process and enable them to enrich their knowledge base and share that knowledge with one another, field workers, researchers and decision-makers at various levels. Internet use among intermediary organizations and leaders involved in participatory research can provide a cost effective method for documenting and sharing lessons learned and research results.

Internet use also has the potential to strengthen linkages between and among farmer organizations extension workers, researchers, policy makers and other actors in a farming system. For example, international organizations such as the Information Centre for Low-External-Input and Sustainable Agriculture (ILEIA).

The cost of accessing printed academic materials within developing countries is usually so high that students and faculty members have great difficulty acquiring books and journals. Also, the time required to obtain printed materials from overseas can be long enough to render some information out-dated by the time it arrives. Via the Internet, information published on-line can be accessed almost instantly and at a small fraction of the cost of obtaining printed materials. Information on the Internet is easy to access and archival lists of resources can be easily reviewed and assessed in remote locations.

Electronic distance education services are already in use in North America, Australia and Europe (particularly among people in rural areas), and with the continued growth of Internet access in developing countries, there is a very good chance that similar services will develop significant demand. Over 87 percent of the rural Internet users involved in the University of Guelph's Rural Internet User Survey indicated that they were very interested in taking advantage of on-line courses and other structured learning opportunities via the Internet, yet there are few such opportunities available to meet their level of interest.

Overall, the Internet holds significant potential to enhance learning and research relationships among researchers, academics and students, wherever they are located. The list of potential applications is infinite and thousands of informal linkages of this sort take place every day on Internet discussion groups. Development agencies can play a role in helping to formalize and provide credentials and diplomas for people who participate in specific electronic learning initiatives delivered via the Internet.

Within FAO's Sustainable Development Department, for example, there are existing training and curriculum development projects focused on communication for development and extension worker training. Other FAO departments and many other agencies have similar projects. The materials and processes created within these projects can be adapted for Internet distance education delivery. Such distance education projects could take advantage of the power of the Internet to facilitate local and international learner interaction and team learning contexts based on group learning projects, as opposed to the traditional correspondence style of distance education.

Small and Medium Enterprise Development

Private sector businesses, large and small, are using the Internet to reach new markets, promote products and services globally, and access critical business and financial information. Rural food producers in North America now use the Internet to sell a wide variety of products including live lobsters and packages of apples, oranges, grapefruit, cheeses, smoked meats, pastries and pies. Producers of rural crafts and manufactured goods sell everything from clothing to furniture over the Internet, and use the Internet to organize support networks. The Internet represents a global storefront for such rural and remote businesses, providing them with a degree of access to customers never before possible.

The tourism sector has been quick to recognize the benefits of the Internet for advertising destinations, tours and holiday services. For all of the countries visited during his recent FAO Internet fact-finding mission, the author was able to make use of World Wide Web travel information from the host countries in order to make travel plans. With full colour pictures, and information on hotels, weather, attractions, events, travel tips, currency conversion rates, visa information and much more, travelers are able to obtain timely and accurate information and make informed destination choices.

Of particular interest are the World Wide Web sites for "ecotourism," game parks, and adventure tours in rural areas of Southern Africa where rural tourism is a growing industry. Tourism operators in rural and remote areas have a difficult time marketing their destinations through traditional media due to production and distribution costs. The Internet now represents a very inexpensive way for them to showcase their sites to the world and interact directly with potential tourists.

News media networks

The news media in developing countries have also been on the forefront of developing Internet applications. Internet service providers (IPS) use the Internet to source news stories from local writers in developing countries and share those stories with international wire services such as Associated Press. IPS is also able to provide Internet feeds that enable African news media to have access to African news from around the continent. This is particularly relevant to rural radio stations and other rural newspaper and newsletter producers that would otherwise have been unable to obtain the same news from other sources. IPS can also provide an outlet for rural news writers to share their stories regionally, nationally and globally. Similar Internet strategies for rural radio networks, which might also incorporate digital audio transmissions, may well emerge in the near future.

Supporting and Development of Internet Initiatives

At the end of the Twentieth Century, people in rural and remote areas of developing countries are facing many unprecedented challenges brought on by the changing global economy, dynamic political contexts, environmental degradation and demographic pressures. The number of food insecure around the world continues to increase. To deal with these challenges, and to make critical decisions, people at all levels of society, and especially the food insecure and the organizations that serve and represent them, must be able to access critical information and communicate. Improved communication and information access are directly related to social and economic development. Participatory development is fully dependent upon communication and information sharing processes.

One cannot expect poor farmers and food insecure residents of rural communities to list computers and digital telecommunication services as high priority items for improving their lives. However, there exist various intermediaries that serve these populations which, together with small and medium enterprises (SMEs) in rural areas, can take advantage of these technologies to improve their work, improve communication capacity, gain efficiencies and reduce telecommunication costs. An integrated approach that fosters horizontal and vertical channels of communication is key to insuring that such benefits are realized.

Intermediary organizations such as extension field offices, rural NGOs, health clinics, government offices, and church organizations together with SMEs, can offer benefit to their rural client groups in numerous ways. Strategies for improving Internet access and use for rural and agricultural development will necessarily involve full participation of intermediary organizations and other rural stakeholders. As Internet services become more widely used among these organizations it becomes more important to facilitate the exchange of lessons learned and best practices that emerge from on-the-ground experience.

The following are the 11 activities to assist rural stakeholders in gaining access to, and developing creative uses for, Internet services:

— Promote regional coordination of Internet strategy for rural and agricultural development.

— Establish pilot projects.

— Use a communication for development approach.

— Support efforts to liberalize telecommunication policies in developing countries.

— Support local Internet entrepreneurs and other service providers in developing countries.

— Assist stakeholders in advocating for Internet service provision and telecommunication infrastructure and policy improvements.

— Orient existing Internet information services to users in developing countries.

— Support rural and agricultural education sector Internet capability.

— Provide Internet awareness building and demonstration.

— Support rural and remote infrastructure development.

— Support creative Internet applications and information services for rural and agricultural development.

Policy and Regional Coordination of Internet Strategy for Rural and Agricultural Development

The Internet expansion in the developing world is led primarily by non-governmental organizations universities, and private sector Internet service providers (ISPs). These organizations are typically small and underfunded, but manage to utilize new and emerging technologies to provide reliable Internet services to civil society at competitive rates. With little or no donor support they have emerged as the most effective and sustainable service providers in developing countries.

Governments participate, directly or indirectly, through the provision of improved telecommunication services (such as fibre optic and satellite backbones), improved policy and regulatory environments that enable private sector initiatives, information and communication technology consulting centres, information and communication technology assistance to the educational sector, and in some cases government telecom Internet service (such as Senegal). Rural and remote regions, however, experience many barriers to receiving the benefits of Internet services. For example, many African capital cities have reasonably reliable Internet services available, but outside such centralized focal points, service is poor or nonexistent.

Donor agencies can play important roles in influencing national policy with regard to rural and agricultural development and national telecommunication improvement strategies. For example, they can:

— encourage governments to support private sector knowledge and communication technology innovations and services targeted to rural and agricultural communities;

— encourage the creation of national information and technology consulting centres, and work to ensure that such centres target some of their services to under served communities;

— encourage national agricultural research centres (NARS) to investigate the potential of national research knowledge systems and participatory research systems via the Internet;

— encourage governments involved in telecommunication service improvement to recognise the needs of rural and agricultural communities for service upgrades;

— encourage governments to involve women and women's organizations in the development of Internet and telecommunication strategy development and activities;

— assist national educational sectors in establishing rural and agricultural knowledge and information systems learning programmes in universities and technical schools, as well as assist in developing innovative rural learning programme delivery strategies such as electronic distance education;

— encourage governments to utilize knowledge and communication technology for administrative improvement, extension, and for civil society liaison within rural and agricultural communities (via existing field, extension, research and administrative offices).

Recently, many funding and aid agencies have been "jumping on the Internet bandwagon" to support a collage of Internet related projects in Africa and Latin America. Only recently have some of these agencies begun supporting coordinated and collaborative activities to support establishment and enhancement of Internet services to rural and remote areas (e.g. IDRC in partnership with FAO in Southern Africa). These areas are, however, the locations with the greatest need for improved communication and information services. Assisting in the coordinated establishment and enhancement of Internet services to rural and remote areas is an activity that donors can support to achieve many benefits for rural populations. In doing so, donor agencies can ensure that their initiatives take advantage of the gains made by other agencies, while serving a sector - the people of rural areas - that may otherwise continue to be neglected.

International Development Research Centre (IDRC) contains a number of useful recommendations for regional coordination of strategy in Africa, including:

— achieve commitment among development agencies to collaborate on a clear strategy for information and communication technology support in Africa in order to improve planning and resource sharing and eliminate the current "overlap in the multiplicity of projects in certain countries and activities";

— improve the availability of information on the existing information and communication technology infrastructure and projects;

— improve access to technical skills;

— improve information and communication technology for African use, which can include non-African knowledge network administrators becoming familiar with the specific challenges faced by African or Latin American Internet users to insure that information available in Europe or North America is equally accessible (in terms of speed and consistency) in developing countries;

— increase support for the development of "local content" and the conversion of existing stand-alone computerised information systems to networked access, integration with decision support systems, and development of new information-based services that exploit local potential; and

— develop and publicise key pilot projects.

Internet pilot projects can enable the development of local applications related to the range of outputs suggested above. These projects should start on a small scale (even small investments of US$18 000 are known to achieve important results) which would allow them to be implemented soon, and take advantage of collaborative opportunities with other agencies. Results should be well documented and shared locally, nationally and internationally via reports, videos, Internet World Wide Web sites, and local and international media. Ties to existing Internet services and projects (urban or rural) that involve significant local participation would improve chances of success. Pilot projects should endeavour to involve women and young people (often the most energetic proponents of Internet communication initiatives) in the planning, development and implementation of activities. Small pilot projects will help establish "best practices," provide avenues for sharing "lessons learned," and act as vehicles for expanding the impact of Internet initiatives and enhancing coordination.

Pilot projects can also document and highlight the challenges of supporting participatory communication for development initiatives. Research on impact not only focuses on users and local applications, but also on people who do not participate directly in local Internet initiatives (perhaps older people or people marginalized from power structures) and suggest mechanisms for enabling them to benefit directly or indirectly from these initiatives. Research can also help provide reliable data on the most appropriate technologies and the essential infrastructure requirements for rural Internet services.

The most effective and beneficial Internet communication and information services are managed and operated by the members of the organizations served. User management ensures that information is appropriate, and actually desired, by local users. Many of the information services currently designed to serve rural and agricultural users are created with little or no collaboration with the intended users.

Non-governmental organizations such as farmer associations and cooperatives, that serve rural and agricultural communities, are best suited for developing and providing information and communication services to those communities. Developing information services with users and catalyzing sustainable user management of communication networks is not a common strategy among funding agencies. It is common to find that intended users are unaware of the information and communication services being developed for them. The FAO communication for development approach helps to develop communication and information services that begin with user information needs assessments, and helps to create system ownership and management strategies that are financially sustainable. Mechanisms for providing training and continuous support, delivered for and by the organizations and users involved, are an important part of this approach. It is relatively easy to install the technology for electronic information and communication networks. It is much more difficult to create systems that people actually use and from which they receive tangible benefits.

Connecting small producers and rural residents directly to Internet systems is, for most residents of communities in the developing world, impractical. However, many of the intermediaries (the non-governmental organizations and government units) that serve these people can use Internet systems to provide better services to the people they serve. Organizations that are predisposed to open collaboration with the people they serve can become focal points for information analysis and Internet communication access. Such organizations can become Community Access Telecommunication Services (CATS), providing locally relevant information analysis and dissemination, together with public access to Internet telecommunication services such as electronic mail.

The latter function is emerging as a service in its own right in many developing countries. The "telecentres" of Senegal and the "cybercafes" (simple electronic mail services and World Wide Web access services resembling old telegraph services) of Mexico and Zimbabwe, developed by local entrepreneurs, are examples of such basic telecommunication services. Basic electronic mail services are beginning to replace fax and telegraph services as an extremely low cost medium for sending messages between individuals and organizations As the Internet expands, various forms of CATS, telecentres and cybercafes will find their niche in developing countries where the purchase of a personal computer is beyond the means of most individuals.

The concept of "community information centres" is not new, but the Internet opens new possibilities for establishing such centres in rural areas. A computer, modem and phone line can place an ever-expanding global library of information at the fingertips of people in rural and remote communities where books are seldom seen. People can gain access to the information resources and tools they need to solve their own problems, set their own development agendas and empower themselves through knowledge. Community centres, schools, rural libraries, local NGOs, producer associations, municipal organizations church centres and health clinics can act as local hosts for community information centres.

CAP offers a relatively low-cost method for introducing Internet tools to rural areas. Community organizations submit proposals consisting of action plans, resource needs, evidence of community support and evidence of matching in-kind and cash contributions. Proposals are evaluated on the basis of community needs and evidence of commitment to local projects. Funding is offered to a maximum of US$25 000, with most proposals receiving between US$4 000 to 18 000. CAP encourages communities to partner with universities, schools, libraries, health care institutions and local non-governmental organizations. People in CAP recipient communities are generally enthusiastic about the project and the benefits it brings. Several communities that established simple Internet services in rural resource centres have been successful in catalysing local entrepreneurs to establish community-wide commercial Internet services.

CAP is a community driven funding mechanism. Projects are designed by community members who must determine technical requirements, appropriate community applications and Internet access locations, together with long term financial sustainability frameworks. Rural communities that demonstrate need and have researched their proposals well are most likely to obtain funding. The CAP administrators provide a great deal of support in the way of information about successful CAP project applications, and the facilitation of horizontal channels of communication between CAP communities. Technical support is the responsibility of the community which must identify the most appropriate level and source of technical support. CAP works well because it is a non-paternalistic, community initiated funding model with few bureaucratic layers between the funder and the recipient community. There are lessons to be learned here for donor agencies working in developing countries.

Support efforts to liberalise telecommunication policies in developing countries Digital wireless telephony has reached the stage where it is now less expensive to build a new local wireless telephone infrastructure than it is to build a traditional copper wire telephone infrastructure. For many people in developing countries, their first telephone is hand held, portable and wireless. In Zambia, for example, by the end of 1997, an enlightened group of local entrepreneurs (led by wealthy farmers) will likely be providing digital wireless telephone service to rural and remote regions of the country that have never had telephone infrastructure. This new technology provides basic telephone service for less capital cost than a traditional copper wire infrastructure, and also enables the high speed data communication necessary for Internet access. Early planning for involving Zambia's main Internet provider,

ZamNet, in this initiative is underway, making the possibility of full Internet access, to even the most remote rural areas of Zambia, a strong probability by the end of 1997.

In other countries, such as South Africa, wireless telephone booths are providing telephone service to rural and remote areas of SouthAtrica, thus providing basic telecommunication service to all residents of the country. Fibre optic telecommunication "backbones" and new microwave and satellite telephone systems are making their appearance throughout the developing world, drastically reducing telephone service costs and dramatically improving telephone service quality and reliability. Internet services are enhanced, or begin emerging, as a direct result of these telecommunication improvements. In many cases, demand for Internet access is driving the effort to improve telecommunication infrastructure.

There is a strong correlation between such telecommunication improvements in developing countries and national telecommunication policies that help liberalise telecommunication services. The Zambian wireless telephone initiative is possible because of a telecommunication regulatory environment that enables private sector initiatives and competitive service. Relatively restrictive regulatory environments in Zimbabwe, in contrast, have so far prevented the release of portable telephony, despite significant demand. Uganda and Ghana, countries in which Internet use is increasing exponentially, have also adopted liberalized telecommunication policies.

The Egyptian Government's decision to support private sector Internet service provision is resulting in an explosion of Internet services and parallel growth in Internet subscribers. Countries which have poor Internet access also tend to be countries with monopolistic national telecommunication policies and little or no service competition in the telecommunication sector. Donor agencies have an important role in advocating for liberalized telecommunication policies that enable competition and the growth of private sector telecommunication and Internet services. It is also important to ensure that liberalized telecommunication environments balance competition with the needs of under served populations, including rural and remote communities.

Some of the progressive telecommunication policy initiatives in South Africa, which highlight the needs of under served populations and rural areas could prove to be useful models for governments around the world (both in the North and South). Local entrepreneurs, progressive NGOs and university computing departments in urban centres throughout the developing world are becoming Internet service providers (ISPs), providing dial-up telephone access to the sophisticated graphical, sound and video communication environment of the Internet's World Wide Web, together with basic electronic mail services. In Harare, Zimbabwe, there are three locally owned and operated ISPs. For about US$20 per month any individual or organization with a phone line can have full access to such a service, to send as many e-mail messages as they like and to "surf" the World Wide Web for hours from a computer at their home or office.

Small business people operating telecentres and cybercafes in urban parts of the developing world (e.g. Mexico, Egypt, Zimbabwe, Malaysia and Senegal) are bringing the Internet to people who cannot afford computers. For less than 25 US cents an individual can use a telecentre or cybercafe to send an electronic mail message (e-mail) to any e-mail address in the world. A simple way for donor agencies to support these initiatives would be to advocate that their field offices and project officers use local Internet service providers wherever possible. Not only will they gain access to better knowledge and communication services, but they will be able to learn more about the local Internet user community and about local development information created by local communities. Furthermore, while it might be tempting for donor agencies to fund the direct creation of Internet service provision and infrastructure, this may not serve user communities well. Donors funding Internet projects would be wise to direct their funds to user communities who can then determine the best choice for Internet service provision. This will help insure that Internet service providers remain responsive to the needs of their clients, rather than the other way around.

Despite tremendous technological and service advances in every country in the world (developed or developing), rural and remote areas continue to suffer poor telecommunication infrastructure. In rural and northern parts of Canada (one of the technological powerhouses of new telecommunication advances), for instance, thousands of people continue to do without basic telephone service, or are unable to utilize existing infrastructure to operate fax machines. Poor telecommunication infrastructure is recognised as an important factor in leading people in rural areas to choose to migrate to urban areas. Rural economic development officers in Canada, for example, rank improvements in rural telecommunication infrastructure as more important than either improved health services or improved educational services, and cite poor telecommunication infrastructure as a primary factor in the out migration of professionals and the difficulty in attracting skilled professionals to relocate to rural areas. They also believe that improved rural telecommunication infrastructure is the key to economic development.

In rural areas, access to communication and information sharing systems can provide simple, but dramatic benefits. For example, the HealthNet Internet service that operates in Zambia is able to provide rural health care professionals with access to medical databases and rapid medical advice from specialist physicians around the world. Such information can literally make the difference between life and death. In Mexico and Chile, rural farmers are able to obtain timely and accurate commodity prices from Internet and fax services, and use this information to bargain for prices from brokers that are 15 to 20 percent higher than they were previously able to obtain (personal communication from a Mexican farmer). Such price differences, within an agricultural system with increasing input costs, tight profit margins, and global competition, can make the difference between a farmer staying in business or losing the farm.

In North America, the poor availability of Internet services in rural areas has catalyzed an important advocacy effort among rural and agricultural NGOs for general improvements to telecommunication infrastructure and policy. Technical obstacles to Internet service have focused attention on a history of government and corporate blindness to the telecommunication service needs of rural communities. In Canada, advocacy partnerships have emerged that have forged alliances between rural NGOs, women's groups, national and regional health care agencies, municipal governments, agricultural producer associations, universities, consumer groups, aboriginal communities and government bodies responsible for agriculture and rural development. These advocacy efforts are responsible for significant telecommunication service upgrades, policy improvements and federal and provincial programmes that support rural telecommunication and Internet projects.

In developing countries, organizations such as FAO can play important roles in championing emerging rural stakeholder advocacy efforts, and assisting rural stakeholders in gaining voices on national and regional telecommunication/ Internet advisory bodies. Special attention should be paid to the involvement of rural women and women's organizations that serve rural communities. Orient existing Internet information services to users in developing countries

The global Internet now provides access to a plethora of agricultural and rural development information and discussion services. Information resources on low input agriculture, commodity prices, alternative crops, international crop market patterns (seasonality of specific regions, crop successes and failures, etc.), new techniques, integrated pest management, rural development strategies, FAO reports and research, and countless other topics are freely available to users around the world. In order for all this information to truly be of benefit to small producers and the people of rural and remote areas, it must be easily available to them and/or to the organizations that serve and represent their interests.

One of the common complaints among Internet users within the development communities of developing nations is that the people at the agencies who provide access to this information via the Internet do not know very much about the difficulty of accessing Internet services outside of headquarters or central offices. The speed of information retrieval in Africa is vastly slower than it is within FAO headquarters, for example. While Internet access is expanding rapidly in developing countries, users do not tend to have access to the same range of high speed telecommunication lines and phone lines that are available in the North. Internet "bandwidth" (a function of the size and speed of telecommunication lines) is generally less in developing countries than it is in the North.

Low bandwidth translates into longer transmission times, and for many users in developing countries, increased costs. As one interviewee told the author "in Uganda it costs US$50 an hour to sit in an Internet traffic jam". One remedy for the bandwidth problem, and one that has a relatively minor cost, is to "mirror" information on regionally located servers that could be managed by local Internet service providers. The service providers could gain some much needed revenue, and local users would have dramatically improved retrieval speeds which would encourage use and analysis of the information that is available to them from development agencies.

Many World Wide Web international development and agricultural knowledge resources are exceedingly difficult to access from within developing countries because they are laden with graphics that transfer slowly across the Internet. This effectively prevents access to the valuable information that lies behind those images. Involving intended Internet information users in developing countries (especially, in the case of FAO, those from rural and agricultural communities) in the design and development of Internet information dissemination techniques is uncommon among development agencies. User consultation methodologies should be developed, and employed as a matter of course, to ensure that users are consulted on an ongoing basis. This will help to avoid user frustration and win user confidence that agency claims to having an understanding of developing country contexts are in fact true.

The most important current Internet user group consists of recent university and college graduates. These individuals are exposed to Internet benefits while at school, and when they obtain jobs in business or government, they encourage the adoption of new technologies and methodologies. Their creative uses of information and communication technology is often adopted by managers and colleagues. Indeed, within any organization one is likely now to find recent graduates leading the way with Internet adoption efforts. Their enthusiasm for the Internet can potentially have far-reaching benefits, and is worthy of development agency support.

In Hermosillo, Mexico for example, three dedicated recent university graduates continue to work full time to provide a valuable agricultural information service despite the fact that they have not received a salary in over eight months. Within FAO's project in Chile, one young woman who recently graduated from a social communication programme, and with no previous computer experience, is primarily responsible for the technical development of information resources currently available to farmer organizations Much of her technical support comes from other young Internet users in other countries with whom she communicates via electronic mail. Throughout the organizations visited during his FAO fact-finding mission, the author consistently found young, recent university graduates playing key roles in the development of local Internet initiatives.

Internet support activities must take account of the availability of dedicated young people, and involve recent graduates wherever possible. Many urban young people, who might not normally be interested in working in rural areas, are excited about the possibility of working with modern communication tools in rural communities. IDRC, for example, is considering developing an international "Internet Youth Corps" to assist in the spread of Internet services in Africa. Activities can also focus on assisting students to gain access to Internet tools.

For the purpose of diffusing Internet services to rural and remote areas, educational institutions in those areas, together with urban educational institutions that have programmes of study related to those areas (e.g. rural development, agriculture, forestry, fisheries, etc.), and research organizations with links to the educational sector (such as national agriculture research centres), could be provided with assistance in acquiring networking computers, training and technical support targeted to young users. Support could also be provided to enable in-course students to engage in practical Internet projects and internships in rural and remote areas. Not only would services be expanded, but local educational institutions would gain a new awareness of rural and agricultural development needs.

In Mexicali, Mexico, for example the university hosting the technical infrastructure for the agricultural communication and information services is now considering offering courses in agricultural communication for development and agricultural marketing. Activities should make a strong effort to involve recent graduates and students in as many ways as possible. Their efforts, creativity, and visions will help ensure success and sustainability.

Despite the rapid growth in Internet service, general awareness of the Internet and its benefits is weak in developing countries. Ties between existing Internet user groups and the rest of the civil society are poor, and there is very little local information content available on the

Internet to help stimulate local interest. Existing Internet services have difficulty marketing the Internet beyond early adopters because it often requires fostering desires and needs among clients who may not know they can benefit from the Internet. Thus, awareness building, through workshops, seminars, training courses, public events and media attention, can help to better inform potential user groups and bring them closer to making the decision to begin using the Internet.

Awareness among national non-governmental organizations (NGOs), and rural development and agricultural extension services, is particularly weak. These groups should be specifically targeted for awareness building initiatives, and it is here that agencies such as FAO can play an important role through their existing relationship with such groups. Findings from the author's fact-finding mission and research lead to the premise that the majority of current Internet users in developing countries belong to one of the following groups:

— recent university or college graduates (both nationals and non-nationals);

— internationally funded non-governmental organizations (NGOs); international development projects supported by major donor agencies; international organizations;

— government units with staff and contacts among the above-mentioned groups;

— universities and the educational sector in general; researchers;

– tourism agencies (government and private);

– individuals within expatriate communities;

— some small and medium enterprises;

— churches with international affiliations;

— physicians, health centres and hospitals;

— communication organizations (newspapers, radio, television); and

— computer and telecommunication companies.

Awareness building initiatives can make use of such existing user groups to provide testimonials, demonstrations and public opportunities to share their experiences with non-users. Groups that are already active in using the Internet in rural and remote areas can provide persuasive information on cost savings, efficiencies and effectiveness, as well as obstacles and solutions to overcoming them. Awareness building initiatives must also travel to the potential user's location, and demonstrate Internet tools within the context in which they may be adopted. There are several ways to accomplish this, including:

— local seminars, workshops and demonstrations with opportunities for hands-on use;

— production and distribution of videos documenting existing rural Internet initiatives, including testimonials from users;

— pilot rural Internet services which can provide longer term exposure. Targeted NGOs, rural development and agricultural extension services provided with public demonstration equipment, and training for staff and outreach persons who can provide specific Internet awareness programmes within specific rural and remote regions;

— enhancing existing rural phone service businesses - "telecentres." Targeted rural and remote telecentres that currently provide telephone and fax services can be provided with grants of equipment, staff training and outreach materials to encourage local Internet awareness and use, and demonstrate the potential for revenue generation and small business applications;

— Internet mobile units which could provide traveling demonstrations and training facilities to rural and remote areas (using satellite technology for Internet connections);

— targeted awareness building for high-level decision makers, whose purview includes rural and remote communities, through in-office demonstrations and "mock" World Wide Web pages outlining each decision maker's scope of services and activities, and including photographs of the decision maker and her or his staff in action with rural and remote clients.

The benefits of awareness building can be accelerated when key decision makers, from both government and civil society, make public statements of acceptance and encouragement for Internet service to rural and remote communities. Such champions can help pull support from uncommitted decision makers and smooth the way for awareness building initiatives. Efforts should be made to identify such champions and support their work.

Rural and Remote Internet Infrastructure Development

Internet service providers (ISPs) in capital cities of developing countries are often keenly interested in extending service to rural and remote areas. However, lack of market research on potential client bases for Internet services in rural and remote areas, and the necessity to take financial risks in providing such services, can prevent existing ISPs (private, non-governmental organization, or government) from building an infrastructure. Where there is good information on potential client base demand, some existing ISPs, particularly those oriented to revenue generation and profitability, are making plans to provide services. Such is the case for rural and remote tourist destinations and mining areas in Zimbabwe (e.g. Victoria Falls) and profitable farming and mining regions in Zambia. A rural and remote connectivity support strategy could contribute to the realization of such existing plans and help expand these plans to provide service to other areas.

Existing ISPs recommend packages of incentives to enable them to take the risks involved in providing rural and remote Internet services. Such incentives could include one or more of the following components:

— low interest loans for purchase of equipment tied to participation in rural service;

— grants of capital for equipment tied to participation in rural service;

— free use of "leased lines" for the first three years of service (user community supported Internet backbones, via land, microwave, digital radio, or satellite, which could be eventually transferred to the private sector for sustainability);

— assistance with the provision of user support, training and awareness building (short term grants for staff in rural and remote communities, access to transportation, and "house call" vehicles and equipment);

— provision of external technical support during startup phases.

Donor funding, is probably best directed at user communities who can then determine the best local strategy for partnering with ISPs. The user communities can then directly provide the incentives for enhancing rural services. Donor agencies could assist in helping to link user communities with existing ISPs and encourage the creation of unique applications on behalf of user communities.

Internet users are fond of saying, "content is king," when it comes to the ultimate value of Internet use. People use the Internet because it provides them with information they need, and the ability to communicate with friends, colleagues, co-workers and peers from around the world. It also provides a communication environment that encourages creativity, expression, enjoyment and experimentation. There are currently relatively few African information services, for Africans, by Africans, on the Internet. In countries where there are organizations encouraging the development of creative information services and applications, African content is high, and general support for Internet activities is also high. Such is the case in Zambia where both national newspapers publish daily versions of their newspapers on the World Wide Web, and host various e-mail discussion groups. Supporting creative Internet applications and information services, particularly among rural stakeholders, will significantly extend the reach of information sharing efforts (locally and globally).

In Latin America, creative Internet applications and information services are developing quickly and there are many organizations and businesses ready to "host" and create World Wide Web information. There are several Spanish and Latin American World Wide Web "search engines" to help users quickly locate information resources. However, information services and applications related to rural and agricultural development are sparse. There is an opportunity to develop a distinctly Latin American rural and agricultural development information service. Ideally, this service would be decentralized support creativity and experimentation, and contain information maintained and updated by many different organizations using a common "homepage."

African and Latin American agencies and NGOs that currently provide creative "on-line" information services report that there are numerous benefits. They report that current and prospective funding agencies find it easier to make contact because NGO information is instantly accessible from the North. NGOs are also able to publicize the value of their contributions within the developed world via creative World Wide Web sites complete with photographs, graphics and even sound and music. Having information on the World Wide Web increases opportunities for recognition by donors and access to new donor initiatives. As the population of African, Asian and Latin American Internet users grows, there will be more and more opportunities to enable Africans, Asians and Latin Americans to develop and share locally relevant information such as extension materials, crop market prices, health information and other information that is poorly distributed due to print publication costs.

There is no shortage of African, Asian and Latin American produced information that can be transferred to the Internet in creative ways. Many national agencies, including national agriculture research centres, extension services, women's organizations, and national/regional NGOs, publish paper newsletters, booklets, manuals, guides, factsheets, and pamphlets, but, due to the costs involved in printing and distribution, these publications may not receive the attention they deserve. Many of these publications are produced on computers using word processing software, and can therefore be easily transferred to Internet software packages for distribution on line. Static printed information can be recycled and gain a new lease on life when mixed with interactive Internet applications that support quizzes, learning games, discussion groups and user responses.

Most existing ISPs rent electronic storage space on the computer network "servers" that can serve such Internet resources to users. They also provide electronic publishing services to clients who may not have the skills to create World Wide Web documents or gopher file archives. A strategy for supporting creative Internet information services and applications in Africa, Asia and Latin America among rural stakeholders can make use of these existing ISP services in several ways:

— grants to agencies, national agriculture research centres and rural stakeholder groups such as NGOs, women's organizations and universities, to host creative information services, library/resource centre resources and information depositories via existing ISPs;

— training in the creation of Internet information services and applications for rural stakeholders that are currently providing information via other media;

— subsidized servers housed and maintained by existing ISPs, but made freely or inexpensively accessible to qualified agencies and NGOs;

— grants of servers to universities, the educational sector and national agriculture research centres to promote skill development and provision of African, Asian and Latin American information services;

— information from development agencies generated for and about Africa, Asia and Latin America (such as that provided by FAO and countless other agencies) "mirrored" on regional servers to ensure faster and more reliable access;

— support for software solutions that enable information retrieval by Internet users who only have access to electronic mail (no World Wide Web capabilities) or who have older computers;

— support for the production and distribution of digital audio (perhaps digital video as well) Internet content for use with rural radio applications, extension campaigns, and development programmes aimed for non-literate populations, in combination with instantly printable graphic illustrations or photographs.

The Internet already represents a vast global library of information that can become more easily available to rural and remote residents of developing countries. Combining existing resources with locally relevant and culturally oriented information can increase peoples' understanding of their own issues and contexts, and increase the rest of the world's understanding of people in developing countries.

7

Radio and Video for Development

Over the last couple of decades we have seen many changes in the use and role of media for communication in development. These have been fuelled from two directions. First, there has been a revolution in the technologies which can be used for communication. Video and audio technologies, for example, have become smaller, cheaper, more reliable and easier to use, making them accessible to many organizations and to individuals, and usable in many different contexts by a wide range of people. Running parallel to this has been a change in development thinking towards sustainability of livelihoods and the participation of rural and urban communities in decision making about their own lives.

Moves towards participatory development and the desire to make development a reality for the disadvantaged, especially women and the "poorest of the poor," have necessarily meant changes in approaches to media: to its role, the technology used, the skills needed, who it is for, and the role of the community and the media professionals.The polarization of media into professional and people-based media with opposing characteristics is now breaking down and being replaced by a continuum of participatory approaches involving different groups of people with a range of skills able to respond to changing needs and contexts. The "professional media" end of the continuum is still with us, but more and more examples are now available which show that there is a wide range of use and users.

Media communication is no longer seen as simply a top-down flow of information, exemplified by the delivery of messages through the national press, radio and television to health and agricultural extension services or to mobilize populations behind government development programmes. Nor are populations regarded as one mass to be blanketed with the same message, but rather as communities with differing needs and perspectives on the world It is no longer considered good enough for media professionals to isolate themselves from the audiences they are supposed to serve. Now they can be found working with local populations to determine their needs in relation to the broadcast media; they are involved with trainers and trainees in the development of training materials, and are facilitating community use of media to explore situations and make development decisions. Their working practices share many of the "salient techniques and characteristics should be considered as elements in a paradigm designed to be useful to community radio projects". These include:

— pre-project research;

— formative evaluation;

— continuing research;

— cumulative evaluation;

— community participation in planning;

— community involvement in programming (content, format, scheduling);

— interaction with community;

— use of local languages;

— indigenous support; and

— interaction with political authorities.

Changes in working practice have been facilitated by the development of participatory methods such as "rapid rural appraisal" which enable outsiders and communities rapidly to share experience and learn together. Where once the questionnaire survey and statistical analysis were the main means of investigation and analysis, there is now a mix of methods which are not dependent on literacy and high levels of numeracy.

For organizations seeking to practice participatory development, in which the development of communicative capacity and horizontal and upward flows of information are emphasised, new technologies that rely less on technical skills and more on sophisticated but easy-to-use equipment can be dynamic tools. Such technologies have enabled non-professionals to become skilled at using media, opening up great opportunities for them to have access to, and control over, the tools for information and communication generation and exchange.

However, although participatory approaches to media have been around since the 1960s and new approaches are constantly being pioneered, their sustained use in development programmes and projects is still some way off. A task for the 1990s should be to "come up with a set of core ideas and principles of participation and communication... ." Such a core set is really dependent on the exchange and analysis of a wide range of practice and experience. Although he was writing of radio, we could apply this to media work across the board.

MEDIA FOR COMMUNICATION DEVELOPMENT

Communication and development theory, provided us with a model for an audience participation approach to designing messages for development communication backed up by a wealth of personal experience, to produce a handbook on rural radio. This has led to the establishment of a Creative Radio for Development network on the Internet. Although there is now a wealth of experience around, and people are starting to share it, we still are lacking a good, universal mechanism for dissemination. The processes of production for a training course based on video by the Agricultural Information Centre (AIC), Kenya, shows what might be called a conventional training institution media unit operating in a participatory way. Their working practice enables them to provide training materials based on short "trigger videos", which help people to examine actions directly related to their working life and, through discussion, decide on ways to improve things. Interest in the use of radio is very high at the present time, and considerable effort is being placed on training in new ways of working. However there are many obstacles which can mean good training goes to waste as the new skills cannot be put into practice. Participatory work necessitates a close interaction with communities and money has to be found to visit and if necessary stay in rural areas. Lack of infrastructure can mean that only those living near roads and cities are reached for consultation and evaluation work.

Radio and video have been part of development communication for many years and their use has changed in response to the new approaches to development and to changes in technology. It may seem obvious, but short-term projects that take no account of the local ability to pay once the project is over lead to dead technologies around the world.

Training remains a critical issue. In relation to equipment there is a need for maintenance and trouble-shooting skills. In relation to use there is a need for people to be able to create as well as use information and education materials, which calls for other skills, and possibly new kinds of training. An approach to training which focuses on job related skills can result in new skills being released into the commercial marketplace rather than being used to benefit the organization or community in which they were trained.

Education in rural and remote areas

Public services, such as education, health care and social security, are virtually non-existent in rural areas in many developing countries, and many countries are cutting back on government spending for such services. In the industrialized world, new technologies and resources for distance education and technology-supported learning, as well as for distance health care (remote consultative networks), are being developed at an increasingly rapid rate. The vision is to develop global or regional resource banks that allow everyone, anywhere, to consult specialists, find the information and learn what he or she needs, when it is needed.

Telecommunications is an indispensable tool for all the above services and activities. "Plain Old Telephone Service" (POTS) would help, as indicated above, but access to advanced services, such as fax, electronic mail, electronic document interchange (EDI) and access to bulletin boards, computer-mediated conferences, databases and ultimately two-way video and multimedia resources would make a tremendous difference.

Radio and television broadcasting, including community-owned and controlled local radio stations, also offer the possibility to bring education and training programmes to isolated areas. Broad-casting also offers a means to promote cultural development and entertainment for people in isolated rural areas. Therefore, the planning of broadcasting infra-structure should also be part of integrated rural development.

Effective international cooperation for sustainable development, ranging from community development and combating the spread of epidemics and drug abuse to disaster relief and global environment watch programmes, depends on the availability of adequate telecommunication infrastructure in the developing countries. Regional cooperation and large scale programmes for sustainable development concerning, for example, new methods of production of energy from waste, development of bio-chemical fertilizers or the promotion of new patterns of consumption, need tools such as e-mail and computer-meditated conferences to share experiences, to involve community politicians and other "major groups" in the decision-making process, and as fora for continuous dialogues on issues of common interest . Also, the thousands of ongoing and new initiatives by non-governmental organizations and individuals involved in community development would benefit tremendously from the possibilities offered by such tools to better coordinate their efforts and to create more synergy. Availability of advanced telematics services in rural areas would enable governments to maintain up-to-date information about climate, health hazards, and other issues related to environment and sustainable development in databases that could be accessed by concerned authorities, organizations and global "watch programmes". Development agencies can only be physically present for a limited time at the site of community development projects. It is becoming increasingly clear that easy access to expertise and "knowledge networks" is essential for development to be sustainable after projects come to their inevitable end. Consequently, the paradigm for international cooperation is gradually changing from dependence on the traditional time- and space-limited "technical assistance" projects to rely more on sustainable collaborative networks.

To introduce computers and advanced telecommunication services in rural communities, where people live the way their ancestors have for generations and are lacking even basic education, may appear inappropriate and too sophisticated. However, if rural areas should be able to compete in attractiveness for business, social and cultural activities with the large cities, rural communities must be provided with at least the same services at the same costs as those provided to the urban population. Arguably, rural communities need even better services to compensate for their geographical isolation and other "penalties" of being far from the cities and markets.

There is always a risk that this will further increase the gap between the "haves" and the "have-nots". Many economists argue that increased competitiveness and profitability of local enterprises will create new and better paid jobs and ultimately benefit the whole nation and improve the living standard of the population as a whole. This, however, will depend on the existence of adequate policies, regulations and legal frameworks that ensure a fair redistribution of wealth and "universal access" to telecommunications. "Universal access" to information and networks would give ordinary people more power because through such networks they can participate in informal, user-driven action groups and decision-making structures, which cannot be controlled by anyone. In the long term, this may radically change the role of politicians and enhance democracy. The main obstacle to providing telecommunications at a large scale in rural and remote areas is not lack of technology nor even lack of money. If there is a profitable market in sight, the huge investment required to build the networks will probably come forward, even though some economists claim that capital is running short globally. True, the cost of providing telecommunications in rural areas is higher than in urban areas, but new technologies promise to make rural telecommunications more cost-effective in the near future. However, a market that can bear the cost does not yet exist, and many countries need to change their policies to create a more attractive investment climate. Access to the "information super highways" is therefore presently an obstacle which must and could be overcome by new technologies, providing there is a market for advanced telematics services.

As indicated above, people in rural areas in poor countries and are quite unaware of the advanced telecommunication services available today and of the benefits of using these services, as are many people in rural areas in industrialized countries. Other formidable obstacles are the lack of skills to use such services and the absence of user support. Therefore, the business of providing basic, let alone advanced telecommunication services, to a few isolated customers in rural areas is likely to be relatively unattractive for still some time.

Presently, it seems that the only realistic way of providing advanced telecommunications and telematics services and the required user support in isolated rural areas is by concentrating such services to a focal point in the community. Even if the service of such a focal point will be limited initially to POTS and telefax, there will be a real need for more advanced services, as indicated above. It is also important to have a vision for meeting those needs that appeals to government decision-makers across the various occupational sectors as well as to telecommunication equipment and service providers.

Just imagine what such a telecentre could do for sustainable development of rural areas and for bringing people in remote areas in touch with the rest of the world. It could be used for data processing, for accessing databases by small local enterprises and individual entrepreneurs. If properly equipped, it could also be used for "tele-training" and for "tele-health care" so that the local inhabitants could learn new skills and get medical advice when needed. Telecentres are also likely to become centres for cultural and social activities, particularly if they are equipped to receive TV and sound broadcasting.

Availability of advanced telematics services in rural areas would not only contribute to reducing the urbanization process, but may even reverse the trend by making it possible for enterprises to locate some of their business in otherwise isolated areas. The community telecentre could very well function as a remote office for "tele-working," shared by several city-based companies. This would contribute to attracting skilled people (back) to the rural areas and to reducing transport of people. Such educated and trained individuals are needed to sustain the process of development and change, once the international and government support required to initiate community development is withdrawn.

The community telecentre could, in geographically widespread and sparsely populated areas, be used as a local hub to which public (and private) telephones located at strategic points covering the area are connected. It could also be complemented with paging systems so that villagers can be notified of incoming calls.

The concept has already been successfully tried out in rural and isolated areas in many developed countries, e.g., in Scandinavia, the UK, including northern Scotland, Ireland, Australia, Canada, Japan and USA. The "telecottage" movement is steadily gaining momentum and national associations of such community telecentres are being formed. Such associations constitute a network for mutual support, through which new telecentres, established in the developing world, could connect with people with similar problems and experience of various aspects of community development.

As indicated above, there are needs for telecommunications in rural and remote areas but there is not yet a "market". Clearly, access to advanced telecommunications has little meaning unless people have a use for such tools. This means that the introduction of telecommunications in rural areas must be done as part of a concerted effort by all concerned government sectors to develop a rural community or region, for example, by:

- supporting and diversifying local economic activities (e.g., by promoting the creation of cooperatives and small enterprises);
- improving social conditions (e.g., health care, social security, etc.);
- improving access to education, vocational training and culture.

Telecommunication development in rural areas will only have a significant impact if it is part of a larger effort of community or rural regional development. Conversely, community development projects are much more likely to be successful if supported by adequate telecommunications.

Development of a community is primarily the responsibility of its inhabitants and of the government concerned. However, a minimum of resources and some external "change agent" is usually required to develop the necessary capacity for community development to "take off". As indicated above, the international community, including the private sector, has good reasons to assist in this process.

Thus, community telecentres must be introduced as part of a concerted effort of community development, in close cooperation and partnership with the community inhabitants, the concerned governments, concerned international and non-governmental organizations, as well as with private sector stakeholders. If community telecentres are to be used as distance learning centres for local people to learn skills relevant to rural community activities, cooperation and contributions must also be sought from the numerous organizations and institutions involved in the development of relevant "open flexible distance learning" resources.

Telematics Services

Information-based services generally do not need a huge investments and information workers do not need years of higher education and/or vocational training to perform their jobs.

It must be kept in mind that users of advanced telematics will nevertheless need to be trained to operate and use fax machines, computers and other terminal equipment and that some people also will need to be trained to maintain this equipment.

Global village

To reduce the rapidly increasing gap between the information "haves" and "have-nots", a massive effort must be made to develop the poor countries' capacity to use these new tools so that they can benefit from and contribute to the global information resources currently being developed at a mind-boggling pace which are available through global, user-driven networks such as the Internet and the World Wide Web. Providing the large rural population in developing countries with access to advanced telecommunication services and develop their capacity to use telematics tools is an enormous challenge. It will require huge investments and a concerted effort of concerned governments, international development and financing agencies, as well as the private sector. Innovative solutions must be found, particularly to the two major problems of access and prohibitively high tariffs.

People in rural areas in developing countries represent large potential markets as well as potential resources, and the task of developing them offers tremendous opportunities for everybody. It cannot be over-emphasized that to reduce the rapidly growing gap between those who have access to telematics and those who have not, action must be taken immediately. This means planning now for advanced telecommunication services in developing countries, particularly in their rural areas, where the vast majority of the population still lives. Community telecentres could be an essential component of such plans. However, this is a relatively new concept which needs to be tried out in countries at different stages of development. Community telecentres are presently being introduced on a large scale in a few developing countries, but the feasibility of this concept in countries at different levels of development still needs to be demonstrated. Appropriate technologies, tariff policies, regulatory and financing options, as well as organization set-up, need to be tested and the impact of telecentres on community development needs to be evaluated to give national planners and suppliers of IT and telecommunication products and services a more solid basis for strategic decisions concerning rural telecommunication development

Video as a Communications Tool

The ability to view immediately one's own self speaking on videotape assists individuals to see themselves as others see them. This self-image conveys the impression immediately that one's own knowledge is important and that it can be effectively communicated. These video techniques create a new way of learning, which not only build confidence, but show people that they can say and do things that they thought were not possible before. For those who cannot read or write, these video techniques make available information that people can understand. They also create new communication links. People can talk with other people in different villages, with other people in different social or economic classes, with other kinds of experts, or with bosses. Video in the hands of a skilled community worker can assist people to talk to other people with whom they may have never before had any communication or access. It can remove the inherent threat in communicating with persons of authority. It can assist in the planning of action and in the resolution of conflict, potential or actual.

The very presence of a community worker with this technology shows or provides a sense of caring and involvement which enhances the willingness of village people to become involved in new ways of learning and doing. The community worker and the video process bring people together for common cause, create new information channels and inspire a belief and confidence in self-help.

There are times, however when video as a tool is inappropriate to a particular situation. For example, the field-worker may be called upon to arbitrate between difficult interpersonal relations within an organizational framework or project, in which using video could actually interfere with sensitive needs which require immediate action. A community worker must be attuned to such situations and know when to make the decision to use or not to use video as a communication tool.

The technology

Video production and utilization equipment that is most appropriate for development workers and educators is not the same as that used for broadcast purposes. It is less expensive and the technical quality of the image produced may not be as high as broadcast equipment; however, community use of video does not require as high technical standards. It is the message, more than its packaging, that is important in community work.

It is important to recognize that there is a wide range of non-broadcast video equipment on the market. This is a highly competitive field, with the technology changing very rapidly and manufacturers constantly developing new models, so great care must be taken to select the most suitable equipment for the purposes for which it is to be used. It is also important to make decisions that are as "long term" as possible. Unfortunately, the video industry looks on three years as "long term".

TYPES OF LEARNING

This is a form of learning in which country residents use their experience and knowledge to teach one another, or member of one community use their experience and knowledge to teach other communities. An example of the use of video in this form of learning would involve the production and screening of a videotape made by farmers in one village to assist farmers in another village solve a problem concerning marketing. This form of learning is informal and in direct response to a community's perceived needs.

Vertical learning

Vertical learning is usually associated with formal learning involving a teacher and students. In community work video is often used for this form of learning to give technical training, or provide information from external expertise. The videotapes are made with specialists in a variety of fields. An example of the use of video in this type of community learning would be the screening of a series of videotapes in the community on the subject of nutrition made by an expert in nutrition from a university or the ministry of health.

Exchange learning

Exchange learning involves the interchange of information, ideas, techniques and knowledge through interactive as opposed to one-way communication. In this form of learning teachers become learner/teachers and those who are traditionally regarded as learners become teachers as well. This process enables the exchange of views, opinions, information and knowledge with a specific objective in mind, such as improving understanding, creating group consensus, and pointing ways to effective actions.

Videotape recording equipment is very portable, making it easy to transport and to use in villages and barrios. It is closest to movies in terms of media advantages in community work. It is light, easier to learn to handle, becoming less costly and has one very important advantage over film: it does not need to be sent away for processing in a film laboratory but can be played back immediately, in much the same way as audio-tapes, on a tape recorder. With video, however, there is a moving image as well as sound.

In the hands of a skilful community worker, portable videotape recording equipment is a tool which can greatly accelerate the process of self-help and learning. As a catalyst for community action, video can assist in changing the human condition as well as describing it. Community workers can use video in a number of ways. One way is to use it within a village to show individuals or groups what they already know. Used this way, video becomes a mirror. It is through such videotapes the community worker can help individuals or groups analyse what they are saying about their own hopes and problems. Video assists village people to look objectively and more clearly at their own statements.

Another thing community workers can do is to take videotapes they have made with one village group and show them to the same kind of group in another village.

Video made with the assistance of the community worker and shown from village to village amongst people of the same background becomes a new form of learning. This is known as horizontal learning and is becoming increasingly acknowledged worldwide as an essential component of education, usually (but not exclusively) among adults. Village people can use video to teach themselves, from within their own village, or between their village and other villages, and they are doing this increasingly.

Vertical communication

Sometimes the community worker and the people use video to speak to people of authority, to people who are regarded as having power over common village people. In like manner, the community worker uses videotape with such people to talk back to the common people of the village. In this way, new communication links are sometimes established and groups and individuals who normally have not been able to talk to each other are able to do so and to learn from each other.

Community worker

Video is only a tool, and it is only as good as the skills of the community worker who uses it with communities. There are some techniques which will help the community worker use video effectively.

It is best for the community worker to get to know well the people in a village before introducing video. The worker must have knowledge of the village, of its joys and its problems, its groupings, perceptions, beliefs and all the things that make it the way it is.

In most villages people have never seen video and it requires careful introduction into community life if it is to be effective as a tool in learning and teaching. If it is successfully introduced it will come in time to be regarded as something of and for the community; if not carefully introduced video will always be a stranger. A good way to introduce video to communities is simply to set it up in a public area, an open space or a location that people can easily reach in the course of their daily activities, and demonstrate it and discuss it with all who are interested.

Usually the community worker will have a small video production crew of two persons at most, who work as part of his team, one looking after the sound, the other using the camera. During the introduction of the equipment to the community, people should be encouraged to look through the camera and to see themselves on the screen. Another successful way to introduce video as a community-controlled tool for learning is to have the community worker and his small production crew videotape non-controversial community scenes which are later played back at open community meetings.

Even though video will be unknown to the community, it is a technology that ordinary people can use and control, and by having the time to become familiar with it in a public setting, they may be encouraged to learn from it rather than to fear it or be mystified by it. Its successful use involves both the screening of videotapes and discussion based on what the tapes have presented. Without the use of a community worker to guide discussion after a videotape has been screened, the technology is nowhere near as useful. In this manner, the development worker and the village people gradually develop a trust for the tool and for each other as they progress in their learning.

Another helpful technique for the community worker is to show the audience the editing process of video technology, to show people that a tape can be erased, or that the content of the tape can be arranged if the people wish to change it to reflect more accurately what they were trying to say.

In order for video to remain an effective tool assisting in community action or learning, people must always be able to maintain trust in the technology and in the people who are using it. The community worker is well advised to give village people every opportunity to be involved in discussing the production of videotapes, in their use and in their distribution. As a good community worker he or she will know that this will take time, as well as much thought and planning with the people.

Methods Videotapes

More than any other medium involving moving images and sound, video lends itself to effective group discussion. Indeed, without using group discussion around the screening of video materials in community work, much of the effectiveness of the technology will be lost.

It is important when screening video in the community to bear in mind two important factors:The showing of videotapes should occur in a place which is acceptable to the community for meetings. In some communities certain groups gather in certain places by custom. These are the places that normally will be most acceptable; but the decision on where screenings are to take place is a matter for the community to make. In some communities where there have been deep divisions, community workers have found it expedient to show the same videotapes and hold discussions in several areas of the community, at least for a while after the technology is first introduced. One thing is certain - children usually crowd in at screenings with adults, and there are not often empty seating spaces.

Videotapes for community use are made for specific purposes. It is important that those for whom the tapes are made should be able to see and to discuss them with each other and with the community worker. The time at which this is most convenient varies from place to place. Such decisions should be left to the appropriate viewers and the community worker should accept the community's wishes in this regard.

Visual comprehension and video

The techniques described here can orient the community worker's use of video with village people and are primarily for audiences that are illiterate and uneducated. Reading instructions or books are of no help and radio often is perceived as a disembodied voice giving long speeches that convey little understanding. When people see themselves and their peers on video, saying or doing familiar things), the visual comprehension for the viewers is so real that in the memory of the individuals, long after the event, the medium of the video may be forgotten.

People may recall that they have actually met with those they saw and listened to only on video. Such reality sharpens the experience, so that the specific content of the video message is remembered for a long time after. This visual experience, especially in relation to receiving information from one's peers, or sending out information to one's peers elsewhere, can inspire belief and confidence in individuals and in the total community. It is exciting to learn that one's own experience and knowledge is important to others and can be an example to others. It is just as exciting to learn that others to whom one can relate have solved problems similar to your own in ways that you might not have thought of.

8

Communication and Social Development: Health and Nutrition

STRATEGIES FOR NUTRITION EDUCATION COMMUNICATION

There has been a complete revision of the concepts, strategies and methods of nutrition education in the 1980's. Typically, nutrition education consisted of little more than "talks" given at health centres. Today, this approach is considered largely ineffective unless it is fully integrated into a broader program of nutrition education with well-defined strategies for communication.The reasons for failure of "conventional" nutrition education have been the subject of numerous in-depth analyses. The "conventional" approach is limited because it excludes analysis of the causes of malnutrition, it makes use of only one isolated channel of communication and ineffective educational methods. It is based on weak unsupported theories of "behavioural psychology". During the last two decades, interdisciplinary teams in collaboration with persons involved in nutrition education field activities have developed new approaches to nutrition education.

First, it is necessary to clarify the frame of reference for the approach to be presented. In nutrition education, there are two distinct situations, namely, patient education and public education. Patient education occurs during personal contact between the health worker and his patient. This is person-to-person communication during which the health worker communicates with an individual in order to improve the parents' or their child's nutritional status.

Public education consists of interventions for improving the health of the general public. Nutrition education is concerned with modifying social communication to bring about middle or long-term changes in the common behaviour of the population. When interpersonal communication forms part of the proposed strategy, it has a complementary role, reinforcing other activities aimed at changing the behaviour of an entire social group.

What is social communication?

It is defined here as that set of norms which determines how individuals of the same culture interact. The modification of these norms is the ultimate aim of nutrition education directed at the general public. Nutrition education consists of interventions into the realm of social communication with the aim of changing undesirable nutrition-related habits. To achieve this goal, a project must be based on a thorough study of behaviour, attitudes and the practices of the social groups concerned. A considerable effort must also be made in the field of communication. Only multimedia strategies, utilizing several chapels of communication, can meet such a formidable challenge. Nutrition education can, thus, be defined as follows: it is that group of communication activities aimed at achieving a voluntary change in nutrition-related behaviour to improve the nutritional status of the population.

Community participation

The participation of the population in the effort to resolve problems concerning them, is today recognized as a necessity by most development specialists. This is particularly important in nutrition education, because it aims at modification of behaviours which are deeply entrenched in the fabric of socio-cultural life. Participation can be obtained by involving representatives of the target population in the planning committees, by their systematic involvement at all stages of planning and in surveys as well as programme evaluation before all interventions. A programme to prevent Vit A deficiency in Thailand was recently inaugurated. The program organizers decided to promote the production and consumption of squash which is particularly rich in Vitamin A. This decision was made only after discussions with the representatives of the communities concerned. In-depth interviews were held with mothers, leaders of the community and health officers. The implementation of these communication activities was left to well-recognized groups and institutions in the community. For evaluation of this programme, volunteers working on this project as well as members of the local communities were called upon.

Nutrition education interventions should not be developed in a vacuum, but should form part of a wider program aimed at improving health and 10,5 nutritional status, within the context of socioeconomic development. Nutrition education should be part of a strategy for development and not an end in itself. The nutrition promoters made important contributions not only because of their work in nutrition but also very crucial was the social communication on nutritional themes which resulted in a tremendously successful project.

Intersectoral and interdisciplinary

The analysis of the causes of malnutrition reveals that a multiplicity of factors conditions malnutrition. Even at the levels of the village community, an interdisciplinary effort is needed. Interdisciplinary work requires intersectoral collaboration because it is rare to find specialists in all the disciplines needed in any one ministry. The multimedia approach in itself requires intersectoral action as the use of several channels of communication generally implies the participation of several ministerial departments. The adoption of a rational course of planning Many interventions in the fields of agriculture, health or nutrition aimed at changing habits, have failed because of inappropriate planning. More development agents now insist on planning by objectives for their projects. Nutrition education is effective only when it is based on an in-depth analysis of nutritional problems and a clear concise definition of objectives and the methods of communication.

Intervention in Social Communication in Nutrition

The scheme for planning nutrition education is based on a theoretical framework, and consists of four phases: conceptualization, formulation, implementation and evaluation. The first phase of the process of planning is analysis. The problem to be addressed must be analysed in order to identify the determining factors to be dealt with during the intervention. Indeed, this is a commonly-held view among promoters of nutrition, and health education projects. It is based on a method called causal analysis which has proven useful in nutritional diagnosis. It involves drawing up a network of factors affecting nutritional status in a given context. This is a hypothetical model on which the team responsible for the implementation of the project will rely, in selecting the objectives for the intervention.

In this model invariably, there are human behaviours, on which nutrition interventions can be focused. The intervention is thus considered educational. It will therefore be necessary to study carefully the factors which influence these behaviours and the habits one wishes to modify. It reveals clearly the factors on which actions must be taken, in order to modify the behaviours in question. Finally, at the end of this phase of conceptualization, it will be necessary to identify the channels and media for communication, the reference and support groups and the social networks through which the messages for nutrition education will be disseminated.

Formulation

To plan a strategy, it is necessary first and foremost to define clear objectives: general, specific and operational objectives. These objectives must be defined for each target group and even for the target segments within the target group. The conceptualization phase and the determination of the factors affecting the behaviours to be modified, greatly facilitates the design of messages and materials. The messages and the materials have to be field tested using methods that require community participation. Support materials cannot be designed until the various media have been selected. Selection of the media is another crucial step in the planning process. It is based on the results of the analysis of potential channels for communication carried out during the conceptualization phase in order to develop optimum synergy between the channels. A multimedia plan is then carefully formulated. In such a plan, all communication activities are integrated with each other.

Is it a priority public health problem?

The extent and the magnitude of a nutritional problem,

groups affected, its socio-economic importance and prioritization as public health problems is determined by nutrition workers on the basis of assessment of nutritional status of the population.

To recall the principal nutritional problems in developing countries: these are protein-energy deficiency, disorders linked to iodine deficiency, vitamin A deficiency and iron deficiency anaemia. A growing number of countries are confronted with new health risks linked to diet. These were until recently the diseases of affluence, namely cardiovascular diseases, diabetes, obesity and cancers. Evidently, the causes of these different nutrition-related problems are not identical in all countries. Consequently, the possible solutions vary especially in that of giving advice to the population.

Since some time, it is known that causal analysis is absolutely necessary for the successful design and implementation of nutrition education. Why is this so? It is because nutritional problems are the results of an interaction between complex and multiple socioeconomic, biological and environmental factors. In all nutritional interventions, educational or otherwise, the promoters must first determine the causes of the problem which have been identified. Beghin et al. have redefined a procedure for the analysis of the factors influencing nutritional status.

The steps in the procedure are as follows

1. Establish an interdisciplinary and intersectorial group including representatives of the population. This group can be the same as the Planning Committee for the project. It can also be larger, but it should then include all the members of the Planning Committee.

2. Once assembled, the members of the group establish a list of the factors known or presumed to affect nutritional status in the population.
3. The group proceeds to construct a chain of causality with linkages formed progressively, and organised into a hierarchy- the result- a network of factors affecting nutritional status. This network is a hypothetical model which will evolve during the preparation and implementation of the programme.
4. The group identifies, on this model, the factors which need to be acted upon. This choice is made, in relation to criteria defined by the group.
5. Among these factors, the group identifies those which seem to be amenable to education: the factors linked even partially to human behaviour.

Factors determining behaviour

Once the various behaviours to be changed have been revealed, it is necessary to analyse a little deeper in order to identify the determining factors. External factors may be economic, social, climatic or geographic. Internal factors have been analysed by different authors. According to Leclercq human behaviour is determined by five factors: motivation, knowledge, self confidence, decision and skill.

— The first factor is motivation. It is the motivated individual who considers modifying his usual conduct. This motivation arises out of a person's perception of the gravity of the problem and the perceived consequences of maintaining or altering his behaviour.

— The second factor is knowledge. When the problem is perceived and there is enough motivation to make a change, it is even more important to know what change is to be made.

— The third factor is self-confidence. This factor is now of primary importance to health educators. They now realize that it is very difficult for people lacking self-confidence to make a change in health-related behaviour.

— The fourth factor is decision, a function of a person's system of values. The person must, choose from among several possibilities, what suits him best (example: a mother who is quite confident in herself might not change her behaviour simply because of other priorities. She may decide not to devote the time needed for preparation of meals for her youngest child. This may not be a priority. Out of the many situations proposed to her, she will select those which are most in keeping with her system of beliefs and values and that of her reference group.

— The fifth factor is skill (faculty of knowing what to do and how to do it). When a person decides to make a change, he tries it out first, but its adoption will depend on try a new recipe to prepare her child's meal will judge from the result of the meal when it is cooked. If the result is positive, she will continue using the recipe but if it's negative, she may become doubtful and abandon the new idea the success or failure he meets.

In nutrition, external factors are of primary importance: food availability, access to health services, and family income are only examples which may prevent or encourage adoption of a behaviour. Among the factors influencing a course of action, those which depend on the people concerned and those which are, unfortunately, out of their control must be underlined. The latter may be such that any attempts to alter a course of action without taking them into consideration would certainly fail.

In any event, it is crucial to understand why people behave the way they do. In general, people have valid reasons (in their opinion) for behaving in a certain way. It is important to discover what these reasons are before trying to make any changes in their habits.

Target audience

The target population for an educational intervention is made up of several groups. In order to adapt the approaches to each group, it is necessary to differentiate between these groups.

Vulnerable Groups and Target Groups

It is important to differentiate between the vulnerable and target groups for intervention. The vulnerable group may in fact be the same as a target group of a communication program, but this is rarely the ease. For example a vulnerable group at risk for protein-energy malnutrition consists of children under five years. The nutrition intervention for reducing this risk will not be directed at the young children but rather at all those involved in the care of children under five years. An effective communication strategy takes into account activities at all these levels. Each target group, especially the primary one must then be divided into its "segments" a term often used in marketing.

Within the target audience there are primary, secondary and tertiary target groups. The primary target group is composed of persons whose behaviour is to be modified. In the example given above, these persons could well be the mothers of children under five years. In that case the aim would be to modify the manner in which they prepare their children's meals or care for them.The secondary target group is comprised of people who will be used as intermediaries to get the message across to the first target group. In the same example, this could be health workers, teachers, agricultural promoters or journalists. It all depends on what the communication networks are in the community.The tertiary target group is made up of people who can facilitate the communication process and behaviour change. There include administrators and politicians but also those persons close to the mother - the father of the child and the extended family.This implies that the approach will vary for segments differing in terms of educational level, socio-economic status, etc. In the last example, we need to differentiate between the mothers who constitute the target group and between the various segments of the target group mothers, which will each benefit from a specific strategy. The media and support materials used to reach mothers who are functionally illiterate and living in rural areas will differ from those directed at more educated mothers living in urban areas.

We must not forget that target groups should be participants in the process of social communication and not mere receivers of information. A one-way communication system for nutrition education would defeat our aim for an effective global approach. Also, the target groups must themselves play a role in transmission of messages to other groups and to the "promoters" of the intervention.

Nutritional objectives

The primary objective of a nutrition intervention programme is the nutritional improvement of the target group. This may be measured by dietary, biochemical, clinical, anthropometric and biophysical indicators. These indicators indicate different stages of nutritional status of a population. Nutritional status is a complex phenomenon which is influenced by many factors external to an educational intervention. The time frame within which different indicators are affected by interventions differ. The nutritional objectives should, therefore, be defined with shorterm and long-term objectives.

An educational programme is basically designed to change behaviour within the long-term objective of improving nutritional status provided the other external factors that influence nutritional status are favourable; for example, improved food production, availability of food and improved health facilities. All these are conditions external to and outside the control of communication intervention. The immediate outcome is the direct result of intervention independent of external factors. The improvement of mother's knowledge concerning the nutritional needs of their children is a perfect example. It is important to set nutritional objectives in measurable terms, but understand that these objectives will be achieved only when factors external to communication interventions are conducive to their achievement.

EDUCATIONAL OBJECTIVES

The specific objective of a nutrition education program is to obtain lasting changes in the behaviours affecting nutritional status. Adoption of new behaviour depends on many factors external to the communication program. Intermediate objectives are those concerned with changes in motivation, knowledge, self efficacy, preferences for a particular behaviour and in the "savoir faire" -the skills required. These objectives are the independent outcomes - the promoters of the intervention must attend to these, in spite of external factors. Educational objectives must be operationalized. This is described in a later section.

Communication objectives

For the communication program to be effective and bring about lasting change, it must focus on exposing the target population to the messages, and on the retention of the messages on their part. In the field of communication, the methods are as important as the apparent results. This is because they forge lasting attitudes among the population. For example, two communication programs can achieve the same objective of message retention. The first program because of its top-down authoritarian approach results in a relationship of dependence while the second which is participatory, encourages the population itself, to make informed decisions to resolve their problems. The second option is to be preferred.

Educational objectives should be operationalized as far as possible. These provide the basis for preparation of an objective evaluation of the intervention. To be operational, an educational objective should state clearly:

— what observable behaviours will indicate that the objective has been achieved,

— who will show the various behaviours,

— what will be the results of the new behaviour,

— under what conditions will the behaviour be shown,

— what criteria determine whether the desired result has been achieved or not.

Specific objective

The mother will introduce between the 6th and 9th month of the child's life, a cooked meal of maize legumes and oil, these being foods which are available and affordable to her.

In terms of skills considerable effort must be made to define the behaviour to be adopted by the population. An analysis is given below of the required practices for oral rehydration, more specifically those concerned with mixing the contents of a packet of rehydration salts with one litre of boiled water.

— Select a container which holds one litre of liquid.

— State clearly that the container must be washed and cleaned.

— Fill the container to the brim with boiled water.

— Open the packet taking care not to spill any of the contents.

— Add the contents of the packet, again being careful not to spill any liquid or salt.

— Add nothing more.

— Stir or shake the container.

— Label the container

— Emphasize that the mixture must not be boiled.

The planning team will be able to define the messages for communication on the basis of this analysis

Media and support materials

To distinguish between messages, media and support materials:

— "message" is the formulation of an idea or concept to be transmitted to a specific population;

— "media" is the channel of communication through which the message is transmitted (e.g. talks at a health centre, school lessons by radio, etc.);

— "supports" are the materials on which the message is transmitted.

Persuasive messages

Well-designed messages reach their target audience. Although there is no one formula for message design, there are several useful guidelines. A selected guideline is given below.

In designing a message, the following points should be kept in mind:

1. Keep it short and simple; include only a few key ideas.
2. Give reliable' complete information.
3. Repeat the idea many times.
4. Recommend precise, behaviour change.
5. Show the relation between the nutritional problem and the recommended behaviour.
6. Make use of a slogan or theme.
7. Ensure that the message is presented by a credible source (as perceived by the target group).
8. Present the facts in a direct manner.
9. Make use of positive expressions, not negative ones.
10. Use humour without being offensive to anyone.

Effective messages

The potential effectiveness of a message is certainly enhanced by format. This concept has been widely used by commercial advertisers so much so that advertisements today are rarely a mere description of the qualities of the product. How can we increase the persuasiveness of a message transmitted through images (symbolic message). Various procedures have been used in commercial advertising and to a lesser extent in public service communication. The reader may consult relevant manuals on communication, marketing and advertising for more information on the subject.

Face to face communication

Oral communication in the form of a face-to-face encounter may take place in two kinds of circumstances. The interpersonal face-to-face situation and the "face-to-face in a group" situation. The voice is the main organ of face-to-face communication but the use of other support materials is highly recommended. These support materials can be printed, visual, and audiovisual. They reinforce the oral communication between the "educator" and his target audience.

Interpersonal Communication, in which two people are brought together in a face-to-face situation, is of considerable importance in any strategy for public education. In fact, the most successful attempts to change nutritional habits have been based mainly on interpersonal communication used in conjunction with other methods.

It was stated earlier that the aim of the intervention is to modify social communication with regard to nutrition in order to change what people say about nutrition. The result of an intervention in nutrition education must therefore encourage interpersonal communication. For the most part this effort has to be voluntary. There is no real compensation for the mother who speaks to her neighbour about the necessity of vaccinating her child.

The most obvious time is during consultation in a health centre. The Health Officer takes time out to speak to his patient listen and help him to find a solution to his problem. This message must complement those transmitted via other channels of communication. Most people working in development programs are involved in interpersonal communication. They can reinforce the messages relevant to the public. The planning committee for the nutrition intervention has to identify these channels and include them in their multimedia strategy.

Communication in a group situation has been the principal means of nutrition education for a long time. There is a significant amount of material available on training for group discussion which deals with methods, group participation and material, and visual or audio-visual supports. The emergence of special supports has led to the development of innovative training methods.

With mass-media communication, the transmitter and receiver are never in direct contact. The interaction is mediated through the visual image, print, or by a combination of these elements.Radio diffusions use sound (music and words). The programmes come in many formats, talks, debates, soap operas, advertisements. Regretably, for a long time health education programmes were limited to debates between journalists and medical experts. Since then a more effective advertising campaign has been developed which makes use of other formats. Radio is a very popular media throughout the world. All countries listed in the "Report on Communication in the World" have at least one public or private radio station. In some of the poorest countries access to radio is estimated at between 2 and 4% of the population, but in most of the developing countries, including Africa, the proportion of radios in use exceeds one in ten. If the population pyramid, as well as collective listening, is considered, it may be inferred that in almost every country, the majority of adults have direct access to this medium. However, there is a need to determine the expected media coverage of the population in the country or region chosen for a nutrition education intervention.

The radio may be looked at from two different perspectives: interactive and non-interactive. The more common way of using radio is non-interactive. Messages are transmitted in one direction, from the transmitter to the audience. Here the transmitter has no direct feedback on the impact of his programmes except through opinion polls. Conversely, experiences with rural radio have demonstrated the possibility of having lively interactions with the people in these communities. With this medium, there is a combination of radio diffusion and direct oral communication with a group.

Television uses sound, moving images and sometimes the written text. Therein lies its strength. However, it is less accessible than radio. In 1990, 38 countries or territories did not have a television service. In many countries no televised programmes could be received in any parts of the country. Moreover the number of receptors per 1000 people remains quite low in most developing countries.

The printed press has its shortcomings. These are linked to illiteracy on one hand and limited circulation on the other. The circulation of newspapers is quite low in most developing countries. The fact remains that the printed press cannot be seen as a popular media but rather as an elitist one. Newspapers can be used in communication projects if the aim is to mobilize a social class comprising opinion leaders and their social networks.Posters can serve as a means of communication. It is advisable, however, to use them in conjunction with other media. This channel associates fixed images with written text, and thus limits the target audience to the literate population. Posters can be used without any text. The procedure is complex and demands a particular kind of literacy skill which most people do not have. The support material for a poster is the poster itself, but may also be in the form of a T shirt.

Select media and support materials

The selection of media and support is done through diagnostic research undertaken in the phase of conceptualization of the programme, where the channels and the active communication networks in the community are identified. The choice is then made with regard to the most important criteria. For example, in a situation where finance is limited, the criterion for cost appears at the top of the table.

In another situation where the problem of financial means is less acute, but where more importance is given to the long-term effects of the programme, the duration for diffusion of the method would be one of the main criteria. The planning committee has to consider which media are best suited for achieving the intermediary objectives of the intervention.

Multimedia combination

An essential element of many successful public education program has been to use of a multimedia combination. This media mix involves an organized concomitant use of several channels of communication. One may speak of synergy if the overall impact of the intervention is increased through the use of several types of media, each reinforcing the other, so that their collective impact is greater than the sum of their influences taken separately. The basis of a media mix is the association of interpersonal communication with mass-media communication. Each channel of communication is specific in its own way. The challenge is to find the best combination which can result in the realization of the objectives for each target group.

To achieve this, the credibility of the message must be assured. In this regard, health workers are often the first choice because nutrition is considered a priority in their field. All the same, if nutrition education aims at promoting food production, other categories of worker may better suited to the task. It is often through communication on a person-to-person level with members from the target community that the best source for the message can be determined. These sources should be identified during the diagnostic research phase.

The other channels of communication can play an additional role in the communication strategy. Radio, for example, can spread the message to a much larger audience than that could be covered by the development agents. Posters can ensure long-term exposure to the message. Today, in many countries, T-shirts are still being worn years after they were distributed to advertise the merits of oral rehydration. It can therefore be seen that the ideal approach is to select not one, but several complementary media to maximize the potential for a successful intervention. This also explains why intersectoral collaboration is necessary. No one sector can control all the media-related elements of the intervention.

Communication support materials

The development of materials for communication usually calls for close collaboration between people who are not used to working together. Each person involved in the task must recognise the limits of his field of competence and be willing to consider another person's point of view. For a long time, people continued to make the mistake of placing those responsible for development of the message also in charge of the development of support materials. Unfortunately, there are few nutritionists who are also creative graphic artists. One can also make the mistake of leaving too much of the design to the graphic or other artist. Professionals and technical personnel concerned with this phase must accept the notion of a team effort where each person's contribution is subject to constructive criticism for the overall good and success of the material.

This is why it is important to define clearly the role of each team member.

— The "nutritionist" is responsible for message content. Nutritionists should make changes in the message if they think that it no longer corresponds to the original idea.

— The "creative" personnel are concerned with design, formulation of the messages and their translation into appropriate materials. They are responsible for the appeal, tone and format of the message and should consider research findings and results of pretests.

— "Technicians" are sometimes responsible for creativity, particularly when it involves an audiovisual material. The producer works with a team of technicians concerned with sound, editing, etc.

— One person should be responsible for coordinating all the efforts. This role is usually assigned to the health education specialist.

— Finally, it is the planning committee who has the power to accept or reject proposed support material after studying the pretest results.

Pretesting materials

The procedures for pretesting materials and messages are similar. Pretesting the message "One drink is sufficient, three means disaster" before placing it in support material is of fundamental importance. It is equally important to pretest the support material before large scale production for use in the field. Pretesting of materials can lead to redefinition of the message.

The methodology for pretesting is similar to that used in collecting data in the diagnostic phase. It should be recalled that focus groups (T.F. N°4) and in-depth personal interviews (T.F. N°3) can be used in pretesting messages and support materials. Interviewing in a central location (T.F. N°2) can also prove useful for pretesting. The investigators go to a location frequented by the target audience and asks question about the relevant materials. The self-administered questionnaire and the legibility test are two other methods often used in pretesting of materials. It is not possible to overstate the need to pretest all support materials rigorously with a sample of the target population and resource persons. Pretesting is usually undertaken before production of school books and, of course, in commercial advertising, but all too often neglected in public campaigns.

Large-scale production

Only when the draft model of the support material has been finalized, should large-scale production begin. The selection of a production unit depends on the availability of resources in the country, district or village concerned. Sometimes, a private company may be selected while in other cases work is left to the production unit of the particular ministry. In a study of the costs of producing materials, the following should serve as guide-lines:

— Development related costs: Fees for the producer (in an audiovisual production) or the graphic artist (for a graphic production).

— Cost of producing the draft model: technician's expenses and costs of materials bought or rented.

— Cost of pretesting: depending on the methods chosen, one should budget for mailing expenses, travelling expenses, investigator's fees and compensation for persons interviewed, processing of data and writing up reports.

— Costs of revising the model: expenses for technicians and use of materials bought or rented.

— Administrative costs: costs related to direction of the program and activities of the planning committee.

— Costs of producing the supports: the market must be scanned to identify the best offer for quality/price.

— Dissemination costs: to be determined when working with the audiovisual media, radio and especially television.

Training and retraining

The training of participants is an important activity which

must not be underestimated. For each category of participants, the following steps are necessary:

— Assessment of training needs;

— Translation of needs into training objectives;

— Finalization of programmes: training sessions, didactic methods, materials, and procedures of evaluation.

Communication Intervention

On several occasions, it was stated that no one medium can, by itself, significantly alter social communication and consequently nutrition-related habits. Interventions should make use of different media which will mutually reinforce each other. To this end, the planning committee is faced with a formidable task of coordination. This is absolutely essential for the success of the programme. Programmes that have been successful in bringing about change in nutrition-related habits have demonstrated the need to complement the interpersonal channel with other methods. Interpersonal communication is a very efficient way of studying the nutrition problem and for adapting the necessary messages. When the development officer has not been trained in active listening, role playing is a good method for developing these skills. In addition to these very personalized interventions, it is desirable to work with groups of people not only to save time and money but also to benefit from group dynamics. The traditional talks before a passive group should be avoided. These are largely ineffective in bringing about changes in attitude or habits. The psychologist Leivin demonstrated half a century ago the futility of this method in influencing what he referred to as "group decisions."

IMPORTANCE OF MASS MEDIA

Mass media are important means of reaching largest number of audience at least cost. They are the modem means of communication, which can transmit educational messages in a very effective way. Television is probably the most persuasive mass media and radio is the media which cover largest number of audience. Their effective use is, therefore. very vital when they are used in a programme.

The school lesson is a special form of media. There is the potential in schools of transmitting knowledge, skills attitudes and values to all future generations of children. In countries where the level of school education is high, the school environment enables one to reach a higher proportion of the population than any other media. Its limitations are with regard to the age of the target population. Children, however, can prove to be effective intermediaries for messages directed at their own parents, or even at the entire community.

Subsequently, programmes for these children highlighted the role that intermediaries could play in transmitting positive knowledge, attitudes and practices to each other, their parents and eventually to the community in which they live. The Programme "Child to Child'" grew in many child-care institutions, especially in schools. Participatory educational methods were proposed, based on the analysis of health problems. Direct Interventions were planned in their surroundings. This methodology revolutionized the traditional academic approach; it made the child the main "player" in his own education.

There are at least two ways of working with schools. The first is to intervene from the outside to educate the children on health or nutrition. The second is to modify the curriculum to include the study of health and nutrition.

The systematic approach consists of using the school as a channel for occasional diffusion of positive messages on health or nutrition. Throughout a promotional campaign on immunization, for example, health workers can explain the program and its benefits to the children. The procedure is quite simple. Those in charge of the intervention begin by contacting school principals. Together, they decide on a programme for visiting schools. During these visits, the teachers allow the specialists in the field to speak to the students. The school resumes its normal programme once the campaign comes to an end. This is one way of integrating school activities in the campaigns. The procedure is simple. It is, however, justified only within the context of a short-term campaign.

The revision of school curricula

The curriculum can be defined as a group of planned activities for education. It consists of definitions of the learning objectives, the content, the methods (including evaluation), the materials (including school manuals) and those aspects related to the training of teachers. If one wants to modify teaching methods on a continuous basis, all these elements in the curriculum must be reviewed and the new objectives and content adapted to new methods of teaching and retraining of teachers.

It is also important to create a positive nutrition environment in the school. Today, it is known that for nutrition and health, the student learns as much, if not more, through what he experiences, than through what he learns. What purpose do lessons on balanced diets serve if fatty and starchy foods are served for school lunch? Why teach hygiene if the children live in an untidy school environment? Principles learnt must be translated into practice.

Nutrition Education" is gradually being replaced by the" promotion of nutritional environment," which involves everyone from the educational community. It is not only about teaching, but also about improving conditions of school life. It is useless to teach the qualities of a balanced diet if the meals served at the canteen are not balanced. The school provides a long-term perspective with respect to change in social communication in nutrition. The messages disseminated at the social centre, the dispensary and elsewhere will find a fertile ground with the future adults of the society, if the school undertakes their training in nutrition from today.

The ideal is to plan for the evaluation of an intervention in social communication from the phase of conceptualization. Causal analysis and preliminary research are part of evaluation. Therefore, evaluation provides a strong foundation for the project. Evaluation can also be undertaken during the phase of formulation of a communication intervention. At that moment, there is still time to reflect, not only on the relevance of the intervention, but also on the order in which the activities should develop, on the expected results, and on the actions that need to be taken before any communication activity. The knowledge, attitudes and practices of the target population have to be measured before the intervention to provide a basis for comparison afterwards. It is never too late to think of evaluation; even during the implementation phase, lessons can be learnt from experience.

1. Causal analysis can help determine the relevance of the intervention. Causal analysis, as presented before, consists of creating in an intersectoral setting, a network of factors which affect the nutritional status of the population. The result is a tool for the selection

of the appropriate intervention, for communication between the members of the planning team and for evaluating the relevance of the intervention. Causal analysis also enables the team to identify confounding factors which can influence the success or failure of the intervention.

2. In the Hippopoc table, inputs, procedures, outputs and outcomes of the intervention are place in cells. The inputs are the elements which are going to be transformed into outputs by the intervention. Example: for nutritional education in the school, they are namely the teachers, pupils, and money invested in the production of the programme. The processes are the activities undertaken in order to transform inputs into outputs. For example: teaching training, the teaching programme produced together with the pupils, the conceptualization and production of school manuals, etc.

The outputs are the results of activities carried out in the intervention. They correspond to specific objectives of the intervention. They are direct effects of it.

9 Media and Education

Television programs, internet websites, feature-length films, newspapers, music tapes and CDs, magazines, billboards, radio programs: essentially, a tool/technology which is used by someone to transmit a message to a large external audience (hence, the term 'mass'). Media is the combination of form (i.e., the television) and content (i.e., the program). Both of these aspects determine the relationship between the sender and the receiver, which with the mass media today is typically one-way, passive and highly controlled.

Like schooling, the mass media is used to support the coercive power structure of a techno-industrial elite (be they corporate or governmental). Like schooling, the mass media undermines our existence as complete and unique human beings, and tells us instead that we are needy, deficient and homogenous. While 'entertaining' us, it complements the education system in urging us to consume and consume to fill our empty selves up. It thus reinforces institutional dependency on professionals and experts, while simultaneously devaluing our creative potential, our hands-on labor, our local relationships, and our own life stories. Like education, the mass media has had, and continues to have, serious effects on our psychologies, our ecologies, and our cosmologies.

Indeed, the parallels between the mass media and the education system are striking. It is becoming increasingly clear that the Mass Media educates; for many people, it is a far greater source of information about the world than textbooks or academics. At the same time, the education system can be seen a form of mass media. Specific tools (curriculum, teachers, examinations) are used to convey messages (about progress and development, in particular) to a large audience.

Moreover, both the education system and the mass media view human beings as 'masses', faceless, nameless, context-less units, who need information to save them from their own ignorance. With so many similarities, it is clear that probing into the violence of the mass media can strengthen our understanding of the education system as well.

Mass Media Is Anti-Democratic

Ironically, the two oft-cited examples of a 'functioning, well-run democracy' - India and the United States - offer us many clues about the anti-democratic nature of the mass media. Part of this is due, of course, to the overall lack of 'democracy' in these countries - given corporations' and international agencies' near-total control over policymaking decisions, highly skewed legislative representation (where one needs to be a lakhpati to contest elections), and low voter turnout. But mass media (television, film, newspapers, textbooks, etc.) helps to facilitate and reinforce these structural flaws. For built into its functioning is a near-total reliance on elite power interests - for management, financial backing, technological know-how, and therefore, for conceptual control.

In other words, what we 'know' about the world is largely a function of what we are told: the often sensationalistic and superficial analysis we get from this monopolized media. Those few large conglomerates who own most of the world's media succeed in diverting public attention away from key issues, root causes, systemic factors, our roles and responsibilities - indeed, everything that is critical for nurturing a democratic society. All over the world, the middle class is kept busy with soap operas, music videos, game shows, superficial news, and sports. By locking us in the passive role of viewer, the media almost guarantees our quiet acceptance of elite power.

In this way, the mass media almost guarantees that people will not reflect on why/how their families, communities, societies, are facing life-threatening crises and what they can do about it. Democratic life is thus neglected. This may help to explain why in Udaipur, as in many other cities in India (and elsewhere), the participation of the Indian team in the World Cup will generate far more attention and action than our local drought situation. This disinterest in our own lives is further exacerbated by the media's promotion of elites.

Experts are propped up time and again to show that we, the viewer-consumers, are incapable of understanding the world, our localities, even our families, without their professional guidance. In the face of their authority, we become silent and obedient. Indeed, the process of 'information-dissemination' by experts leaves us feeling isolated and weak, incapable of doing anything to stop/ change the massive machines of government and business.

To establish the rule of the expert elites, media is used to deliberately and conveniently blur the line between 'fact' and 'interpretation'. Subjective/biased analyses are passed off as the objective Truth - not to be doubted in any way. If one dares to raise a question, they are quickly labeled either anti-national or a terrorist. In India, the 'closing of the ranks' occurs most often around the issue of Kashmir. If one disagrees with the Government of India's plans and procedures, they must be unpatriotic and pro-Pakistan. This false sense of 'objective' analysis is one of the greatest threats to democratic thinking and living. It allows the mass media to complement the indoctrination we received in schooling, to constantly submit to the experts' version of the Truth.

In addition, the near-total reliance on advanced technologies (satellites, computers, cameras) ensures that the majority of the world's people will never be able to participate in the creation or control of mass media. Both the access to the technology itself and/or the knowledge needed to operate the technology is limited to a select few throughout the world. This alienation from (and yet simultaneous dependency on) technology aggravates the already undemocratic nature of the mass media.

Mass Media Is Anti-Expression

In form and content, the mass media also silences our individual and collective expressions. It does this first and foremost by devaluing our own lived experiences. Who we are, how we live, how we express ourselves, is nothing in comparison to the images we are shown and the commentaries we are given about 'reality'. Those are assumed to be more important and more honest than our own lives. The media's obsession with celebrities, from Shah Rukh Khan to Sachin Tandulker, serves to remind us how boring our own lives are. Yet, it is only through engagement with our own experiences that we come to understand our concerns, fears, dreams, and hopes. These understandings are then expressed in various forms, such as dance, music, painting, sculpture, poetry, stories, farming, weaving, friendships, worship, etc.

Interestingly, we can look at these expressions as media also, in another sense of the term - as meaning-making, idea-sharing, feeling-communicating. This kind of media differs from television, the internet, newspapers and other mass media, in several ways: First, in who gets to create/conceptualize them. Expressions can be generated by everyone, because they are rooted in the self, culture and nature. Their creation therefore cannot be owned by any one group or centralized in one space or time. No one, for example, has a monopoly on making music or creating a work of art. However, the mass media, as described above, is produced by a small group of elites, who maintains control over the ideas/values/perspectives offered.

Second, expressions differ from the mass media in how they are made, used and viewed. Because expressions come from the heart, within a local context, they are typically low- or no-cost (in terms of the modern cash economy) and utilize convivial technologies (natural colors, simple tools, etc.). Those who live in that locality interact with these kinds of expressions, which means that they remain close to most peoples' daily lives, their families, their feelings and their work. Good examples of this 'small media' are generated every day (in relation to food and crafts), as well as during special occasions like Rakshabandhan, Holi, Sakranti, weddings or other celebrations.

In contrast, the awesome and expensive technological grandeur of the mass media ensures that only a few can be involved in making it. And although it is disseminated to many (like compulsory schooling), in doing so, it promotes the notion that authority and 'right answers' are far more important than the particularity of a person's life, story, feeling, wisdom, etc. The scale and size of the mass media thus effectively kills self-esteem, creativity, responsibility, diversity, which are the building blocks of local expressions.

Mass Media Is Anti-Human

If we understand the undemocratic and anti-expressive nature of the mass media, then we begin to see what a great affront to our own humanity it is. In essence, the mass media projects (in brilliant color) the culture of competition, profit and material growth above all else, which is crushing the world today. It aligns with the dominant political economy to try and convince us that this kind of Development is the only possibility for the present and the future. "This path is inevitable," it proclaims - and so we should all play the game to win. Winning, on its terms, means greater consumption of market services and products, and greater submission to the state: "Don't raise questions about India's nuclear policy, or the death of small farmers and artisan communities, or the lack of water in your area, or your family's breakdown, or your own anger and depression. Instead, have a Pepsi-Cola, buy a lottery ticket, and keep trying to win (i.e., fit into this system)."

This dehumanizing attitude is largely due to advertising - by far, the dominant feature and function of the mass media. Indeed, without advertising, the mass media could not exist. Advertising seeks to remind us how sad and needy we are, how incomplete and imperfect. And after showing us our problems, it also gives us the solution: we can attain happiness and wholeness, by purchasing the right Toyota motorcycle, or Lakme cosmetic, or Cadbury candy. Advertising, of course, is made more potent by the format of mass media. Like schooling, the mass media is physically-isolating, psychically-numbing, and disconnected from real life interactions and context. We are alone when we watch television or read the newspaper. The format thus guarantees that messages are transmitted one-way, from external authorities to passive/silent viewers. All of this combined leaves us ripe to follow the advertisers' messages.

In this way, the mass media (like education) helps to produce self-serving, de-humanized units, cut off from one another and dependent on massive institutions for their thoughts, values and actions. This makes it a powerful tool for social control and indoctrination, and enables it to reinforce the unjust status quo (the 80-20 divide in society, in which 80% of wealth/resources are controlled by 20% of people).

Challenging the Mass Media

Perhaps the initial response to the above analysis (at least, from the Right) will be to privatize the media, remove it from the State's hands and give it to private interest groups, who will make it more free and democratic. The problem is that this solution does not challenge the underlying logic of the mass media, which is as follows: the media has to be Big and run by experts, to be meaningful or important. To be Big, it requires large amounts of money and an impressive management to run it. Whoever has this money, or is selected for this management, will therefore own and operate the media. Which today means either the State or Market will be in control.

The problem is, accountability from both the State and the Market is improbable or even impossible. Incidentally, we need to do the same thing for learning. It is time to question the perverse logic that learning is scarce and can only happen in schools (which therefore will be owned and managed by either the State or by Corporations). If we see that learning (like media) is in each of our hands, we will not only challenge current levels of indoctrination and manipulation, but we can also free our creative and expressive potentials.

A second response of critics may be that what is needed is a more democratic and progressive system of media which brings in the voices of all people and addresses the key issues of our times. This can either come about by making the existing model 'freer' or by setting up a new alternative mass media (like an alternative education system). Yet, if that alternative system still needs to be Big, still needs experts, still requires a lot of money and technology, and still intends to 'educate' and 'inform' the masses, then it will essentially replicate the undemocratic, anti-expressive and dehumanizing effects of the current mass media. That is, so long as the format and underlying assumptions remain, then no matter what the content, the media will continue to be a tool for elite power interests.

For this to happen, media (like learning) ought to be considered in its expanded sense, as meaning-making, idea-sharing, feeling-communicating... This enables it to be small scale, diverse, and creative. Which means each individual, in each locality, can generate many, many different forms of such media, to be shared with other individuals and other localities. This is already happening all over the country, particularly in places where mass media and schooling are limited in scope.

PRINT MEDIA IN EDUCATION

Print is the most common medium used in education. Forms of print are textbooks, manuals, course notes, and study guides. Print materials are relatively inexpensive to develop or distribute. Print is used in some form by almost all education courses, regardless of what other media they employ.

Print is the foundation of distance education and the basis from which all other delivery systems have evolved. The first distance-delivered courses were offered by correspondence study, with print materials sent and returned to students by mail. While technological developments have added to the repertoire of tools available to the distance educator, print continues to be a significant component of all distance education programs.

Advantages

— *Spontaneous.* Print materials can be used in any setting without the need for sophisticated presentation equipment.

— *Instructionally transparent.* The medium of delivery should enhance, not compete with, the content for the learner's attention. If the student reads well, the print medium is the most transparent instructional medium of all.

— *Non-threatening.* Reading is second nature to most students. As a result, they are easily able to focus on the content, without becoming mesmerized or frustrated by the process of reading itself.

— *Easy to use.* Given adequate light, print materials can be used any time and any place without the aid of supplemental resources such as electricity, viewing screen, and specially designed electronic classrooms. The portability of print is especially important for rural learners with limited access to advanced technology.

— *Easily reviewed and referenced.* Print materials are typically learner-controlled. As a result, the student rapidly moves through redundant sections, while focusing on areas demanding additional attention.

— *Cost-effective.* No instructional tool is less expensive to produce than print. In addition, facilities abound for the inexpensive duplication of these materials.

— *Easily edited and revised.* In comparison to technically sophisticated electronic software, print is both easy and inexpensive to edit and revise.

— *Time-effective.* When instructional print materials are created, the developer's primary focus remains on content concerns, not the technical requirements of the delivery system.

Limitations

— *Limited view of reality.* Print, by its reliance on the written word, offers a vicarious view of reality. Despite the use of excellent sequential illustrations or photos, for example, it is impossible to adequately recreate motion in print.

— *Passive and self-directed.* Numerous studies have shown that higher learner motivation is required to successfully complete print-based courses. To a certain extent, the passive nature of print can be offset by systematic instructional design that seeks to stimulate the passive learner. Still, it takes more motivation to read a book or work through a written exercise than it does to watch a television program or participate in an audioconference with an instructor encouraging student participation and response.

— *Feedback and interaction.* Without feedback and interaction, instruction suffers, regardless of the delivery system in use. By nature, print materials are passive and self-directed. Even with print materials incorporating feedback mechanisms and interactive exercises, it is easy for learners to skip to the answer section.

— *Dependent on reading skills.* Thanks to television, most students have developed fairly good viewing skills by age four. These same children, however, often fail to develop adequate reading skills by age 12. Reading skills must often be improved. Lack of ability in this area cripples the effectiveness of even the most instructionally sound print material and must be overcome if print is to be used effectively.

Formats of Print Materials

Various print formats are available, including:

Textbooks. As in traditionally delivered courses, textbooks are the basis and primary source of content for the majority of distance-delivered courses. While textbooks should always be critically reviewed before adoption, this is especially critical when the learner and the instructor are not in daily contact.

Study guides. Typically, distance educators use study guides to reinforce points made during class and through the use of other delivery systems. They will often include exercises, related readings and additional resources available to the student.

Workbooks. In a distance education context workbooks are often used to provide course content in an interactive manner. A typical format might contain an overview, the content to be covered, one or more exercises or case studies to elaborate the points being made, and a quiz or test (with answer key) for self-assessment. In addition, there is typically some form of feedback, remediation, or "branching" loop to recycle students through the instruction as needed.

Course syllabus. A comprehensive and well-planned course syllabus is the foundation of many distance-delivered courses. It provides course goals and objectives, performance expectations, descriptions of assignments, related readings (often by session), grading criteria, and a day-by-day overview of the material to be covered. The syllabus must be as complete as possible in order to guide the students through the course in the absence of daily contact with the instructor.

Case studies. If written imaginatively, case studies are an extremely effective instructional tool. In fact, case studies are often designed around the limitations of print and intended to spark the students' imaginations as they place themselves in the particular case under consideration. Many case studies present a content-based scenario. They raise questions, pose alternative solutions, and then branch students to different sections of the text. There, the consequences of the selected alternative are described.

Designing Instructions

Because print is largely a one-way communication medium, the challenge is to design instruction to maximize the amount of interaction in distance education print materials. Consider:

Writing style. Misanchuk suggests that distance educators write instructional materials with language more like that used for speaking than for writing journal articles or books. His tips for writing instructional materials include:

— Use short sentences.

— Avoid compound sentences.

— Avoid excess information in a sentence.

— Use the active voice.

— Use personal pronouns.

— Keep equivalent items parallel.

— List conditions separately.

— Avoid multiple negatives.

— Use point form.

— Use familiar examples.

— Write as you would speak.

— Avoid unnecessary and difficult words.

— Avoid jargon; use technical terms only when necessary.

Put sentences and paragraphs into a logical sequence: first things that affect many, then things that affect few; first the general, then the specific; first permanent provisions, then temporary ones.

Avoid cultural and gender stereotyping.

Focusing on content organization before developing content. Prior to content development, create an outline of the material to be covered. Print materials are often too wordy because the author is planning, organizing and writing at the same time. Instead, organize content based on the identified goals and objectives. At first, focus on systematically and creatively ordering the flow of topics, not polishing a finished product. The end result will be a well-organized content outline from which the written content will easily flow.

Developing a course introduction. Misanchuk suggests developing a written course introduction that will be the very first thing a distant student sees. The course introduction can include biographical background information about the instructor, a course overview, course goals and aims, a listing of any textbooks or ancillary learning materials that will be needed, and information about assignments, examinations, and grading.

Staying with a consistent format. Learner anxiety with the unknown can be reduced through consistency in instructional presentation. Develop an effective format and organizational scheme and stick with it. Use adequate headings and subheadings to visually guide the reader through the material.

Using advance organizers. Advance organizers are a means to connect new material with a learner's prior knowledge and cognitive structure. They should be of a more general and abstract character than the learning matter that follows and help the learner to relate different parts and concepts of teaching material to each other. Place the most general and comprehensive ideas at the beginning of a lesson and progress to more structured and detailed information.

Using examples and analogies. In a traditional classroom, teachers spontaneously provide examples and analogies to illustrate a point that students are having difficulty understanding. Because distant students and their teachers may not have this type of interaction, include lots of good examples and analogies in print-based materials. Be sure, however, that these examples address the various cultural groups, ages and experiences of the students.

Including questions. Questions in print material can stimulate the learner to be more active and to deal more intensively with the learning matter. Use questions that aim at understanding rather than merely reproduction and memorization of facts.

Adding a table of contents. A detailed table of contents can help the learner to quickly refer to the appropriate section.

Incorporating a glossary of terms. A glossary summarizes all the new, often technical terminology encountered in a document. It may be helpful to delineate glossary entries in the instructional material by putting them in boldface type.

Broadcasting Media in Educational Purposes

Radio and television broadcasting has been used for educational purposes for many years. There are different types of broadcast: public, cable, and satellite. Some of the advantages of radio and television broadcasting is that they Audio- and videotapes have come to play an increasingly important role as media for distance education. These technologies are convenient and cost-effective. Most people have VCRs in their homes, and videotapes are easy and inexpensive to distribute. These media can be used to present the views of experts, which would increase the credibility of and interest in the materials. Materials that cannot be communicated by print could be communicated this way. Video is a powerful medium in terms of capturing attention, and conveying a lot of information quickly.

Producing audio- or videotape helps keeping students in track, and get people in the community involved, and may recruit new learners to the institute. Broadcast may be provided to learners through cable television network or satellite broadcast. Those channels can provide good quality broadcast and dedicated channels for educational purposes.

Audio Media

The genesis of many audio media, for example magnetic recording tape, phonographs, tape recorders and microphones, can be traced to the mid and late 19th Century. Inventors such as Thomas Edison, Leon Scott, Alexander Graham Bell, Charles Pathé, Fritz Pfleumer and Valdemar Poulsen are credited with pioneering the first audio media. Following years of technological refinement, initial applications for these media were found within the spheres of government, business and entertainment. The advent of instructional applications of these media gave rise to the term 'instructional media', which Wilbur Schramm points out is '... simply the media of communication used for teaching and learning. Only the use is different. 'In an attempt to categorize instructional media that greatly contrast in development and delivery costs, Schramm called complex, expensive media such as television and computer-assisted instruction 'big media' and the less expensive to produce and easy to use media such as slides or overhead transparencies 'little media.'

Some distance educators have been captured in the eye of the technological tornado and often correlate the use of sophisticated big media technologies with more successful learning outcomes. This is not to say there is no place for sophisticated media in distance education: in certain circumstances big media are necessary. The alluring qualities of complex media such as television and computer-assisted instruction (CAI), however, often determine which medium is employed rather than delivery and pedagogical implications.

Within the context of distance education, audio can be seen as the 'big-little medium'. Though print remains the base medium for most distance education curricula, audio, in a multitude of formats, is highly used though often undervalued. A common assumption among distance educators is that the term 'audio' refers only to audio cassettes or radio. Although these two modes of delivery are very common in distance e ducation, we must not forget how widely used and how vital other modes of delivery are as well.

Film, video, broadcast television, audio and video teleconferencing and some computer-assisted instruction (CAI), employ audio as an integral medium. Thus, audio is used in many multi-media formats and plays an essential role in most non-print media developed for distance education. With audio cassette or radio delivery modes, audio stands alone and may be categorized as 'little media.' However, when audio is combined with varying modes of visual presentation (i.e. film, video, videodisc) and is delivered by expensive hardware, it can be categorized as an integrated component of big media.

The advantages of the audio cassette, and the intrinsic flexibility of this delivery mode within the context of design, production and delivery, will be discussed. The question of media selection for distance edu cation and other aspects of audio such as radio, digital audio and teleconferencing will also be addressed.

Advantages

Media such as film, video, and broadcast television that employ an audio component possess two common characteristics. First, they are all multimedia formats that utilize a visual component and an audio component. Second, the audio and visual components are physically interlocked.

One great advantage of the audio cassette is that it can be designed to be used on its own or with visuals. In the latter scenario, the user and developer can review or preview each medium independently because they are not physically interlocked. This type of flexibility satisfies one of the important criteria of distance education by offering maximum learner control over the media. Referring to first year mathematics students' use of audio cassettes with printed visuals at the British Open University, Mason and others say, 'Our students have responded extremely posit ively with high usage (comparable to straight print), repeated stopping and going back, and they have experienced great pleasure at the use of a friendly voice'.

Another advantage of the audio cassette is the number of traditional production styles that can be employed. For example, drama, documentary, docudrama and narratives may be used in any number of disciplines. The Open Learning Institute in British Columbia has used a wide range of traditional and many non-traditional production styles in hundreds of audio programmes. Only audio can reproduce authentic aural stimuli. The two most common forms of aural stimuli are the spoken word and music.

The average human voice has the ability to produce sound over a specific range of frequencies. The ability to adjust or modulate these frequencies allows us to communicate in a correct and artistic way with words and sounds. The ability to adjust intonation, inflexion, phrasing, pacing, volume, loudness and tim bre 'distinguishes a spoken text from a written one and ... can provide it with educational advantage'. If, for example, learning objectives that emphasize feelings or emotions have been identified, spoken words through heightened intonations or subtle nuances can communicate those emotions and create a sense of intimacy at the same time. Print does not allow a learner to identify or interpret audible nuances that personalize content because print cannot stimulate the auditory senses.

Another advantage of the spoken word is its ability to communicate the rhythms, tempos and inflections of languages. The Open Learning Institute offers three language courses that include 39 audio cassettes. A distance education learner would encounter great difficulties attempting to learn a new language from print materials without a corresponding audio component. 'As compared with a written text, the spoken word can influence both cognition (adding clarity and meaning) and motivation (by conve ying directly a sense of the person creating those words)' says the Open University's Nicola Durbridge. Other courses at the Open Learning Institute, such as English Literature, English Grammar, Science, and English as a Second Language take advantage of audio's ability to replicate aural stimuli.

Music on audio cassettes is used in a variety of ways by many distance education institutions. At the Open Learning Institute, most of the audio programmes use music in some of the following ways:

— as an attention-getting device at the beginning of a programme;

— as a theme or an audible signature;

— suggesting a place;
— suggesting locale;
— heightening mood or atmosphere;
— punctuating speech or dialogues;
— as a sound effect; and
— as links and bridges between segments of instruction.

As with the spoken word, music is best communicated by media that can successfully exploit all its inherent attributes. For example, in a self-directed setting, pri nt alone is not capable of communicating the energy or emotion of music. As with language instruction, it is both instructional design and the medium of delivery that influence learning when undertaking musical instruction. With musical instruction, as opposed to musical accompaniment, the message is dependent on a medium that can replicate authentic stimuli.

That music accompaniment may influence motivation or increase learning is uncertain because little research has been done in this area. However, in a survey of current research on the 'Contributions of Music to Media', Steven Seidman suggest that, 'Although it seems unlikely that musical accompaniment to media productions will improve student performance on achievement tests or enhance learning and retention of cognitive content, the studies cited in this review suggest that affective and cognitive interpretations of these productions can be influenced by a musical score'.

Therefore it is possible that the cumulative psychoacoustic (the sensations produced by sound), psychological and physiological effects of music do influence cognition and motivation when the music is the message. And music may influence affective and cognitive interpretations when accompanying other messages.

Other important advantages of using audio cassettes for distance education are as follows:

— the eye can focus on printed materials while being guided by the audio cassette (pedagogical);

— a learner's hands are free to perform activities while listening to the audio cassette (pedagogical);

— the record/playback hardware for audio cassettes is often much easier to operate than video equipment, and computer software and hardware (accessability);

— it can be much less expensive to produce a finished audio programme for distribution by cassette than producing a film, video or a broadcast television programme of equal length (cost);

— there are no time restrictions imposed on programmes distributed by audio cassett es such as those imposed on broadcast media (flexibility);

— unlike broadcast media, audio cassettes can be listened to at any time of the day (accessibility);

— the learner has complete control over all the record/playback hardware which is not the case for broadcast media (learner control);

— audio cassette recorder/players are less expensive and are often more accessible to distance education learners than video recorder/players, televisions or computers (cost/accessibility);

— blank audio cassettes cost less per unit than any format of video cassettes (cost); and

— compared to video cassettes, audio cassettes are less expensive to duplicate, package and deliver because of high-speed duplication, and the low cost of hardware, labour, materials and mailing (cost).

There are many distance education and other agencies-for example, Canada (Athabasca University, Téléuniversité, Québec), China (Central Broadcasting and Television University), United Kingdom (Open University), and Thailand (Sukhothai Thammathirat Open University) to name a few-that broadcast educational radio programmes. Many successful applications of radio have been found for developing nations. A good example is the use of radio for the in-service training of teachers through radio and correspondence in Keyna by the Correspondence Course Unit, in the Institute of Adult Studies, University of Nairobi. By using radio and printed materials, prospective teachers in Kenya could continue working while they obtained academic and professional qualifications. Because radio was accessible to most of the population, it became an important catalyst in fulfilling the training needs of desperately needed teachers at that time.

One of the most exhaustive studies examining the use of radio by a distance education institution was undertaken by Bates and others at the British Open University. Among other issues this study, titled 'Radio: The Forgotten Medium?', looked closely at the value of radio at the UKOU. But perhaps the most interesting aspect of this study was the comparison of the educational economic benefits between audio cassettes and radio. The results of the study clearl y indicate that audio cassettes are favoured by both instructional developers and learners. The study identified four main reasons 'why audio cassettes seemed to be more favoured rather than radio':

1. The involvement of academics in the design of audio cassettes increased. Academics believe that it is easier to integrate audio cassettes than radio into the design of textual materials because of the learner's ability to stop the cassette, work on the printed components and return to the cassette for further instruction.
2. Learners see cassettes as more personal and informal than radio.
3. Learners are able to listen to a cassette at any time as opposed to scheduled radio programmes.
4. For controlled, didactic teaching it was found that audio cassettes are more appropriate than radio.

It was also found that the number of course enrolments often determines whether audio cassettes or radio can be used to deliver an audio component (note that audio cassettes and radio were both used in a number of courses). One of the important factors here is the cost of radio transmission time versus the cost of duplication and mailing audio cassettes. Though these are very important factors, other institutions will have unique cultural, geographic and economic considerations that may ultimately determine which medium is feasible for delivering audio programming. These findings support the argument that audio cassettes are a flexible medium for distance education. But the study also identifies the benefits of radio programming at the UKOU:

1. Courses that use audio cassettes may require up-dating of certain material. They may also require addressing contemporary issues of some relevance to the course.
2. Radio may be used for enriching courses, particularly Arts courses.

3. Radi o can be used as an effective publicity vehicle for general institutional promotion, specific programmes and specific courses.
4. Radio offers the opportunity to transmit general interest programming which effectively heightens the awareness of the population.

The one aspect of radio that has the potential of affecting all others is the ability of an institution to transmit programming at appropriate times to its listening audience. Transmission times should accommodate the majority of learners' lifestyles and allow for pre- and post-transmission course work. If listening to radio broadcasts becomes too inconvenient for learners because of unreasonable transmission times, the merits of using this medium could rapidly decline.

Telecommunications offer a vast number of practical and innovative opportunities for audio in distance education. The telephone tutoring system, for example, is used by many distance education institutions. In many countries, audio t eleconferencing is becoming more and more accessible to all sectors of society and offers specific advantages such as the ability to interact with a large group of people at the same time, the ability to disseminate course specific errata or other information to a specific audience, and the ability to interact in a 'live' format with large groups of people at less cost than interactive video conferencing. Other interactive telecommunication systems are being investigated which allow interfacing between computers and audio. These are presentations that typically use computer graphic templates and static graphic images with a 'live' audio component such as an instructor who can interact with learners over telephone lines.

Importance of Television in Education

On a limited basis, computers with the appropriate electronic circuitry are now able to produce spoken words. The term used to describe this is 'speech synthesis.' Phillip Barker explains the various types of speech synthesis currently available. The possibilities for speech synthesis in distance education are many. For example, if an institution that houses a mainframe computer possessed voice synthesis processors and software, learners with appropriate equipment could access these programmes via a telephone interface or modem. This accessibility could benefit learners in many ways: they could use this feature at any time of the day; they could hear the pronunciation of difficult words that appear in their printed course materials; and, as with audio cassettes, they could review audio components such as those designed for language instruction as often as they deemed necessary.

For these various reasons use of television has been increasing from day to day by a large audiences. It makes television inevitable in the practice of distance education field in Turkey as a developing country. From the point of the faculty, television broadcast can reach a large audience across the country through its national network. The faculty can also make use of newer, synchronous technologies or use interactive technologies such as teleconferencing, internet services, etc. Using of these technologies should take into account the target community. In other words, the best technology to provide all individuals equal opportunities is radio-television technology. This is the main reason that television, a more advantageous technological tool than radio with its audio-visual facilities, is being used non-stop and is improving in each project of the Open Education Faculty.

Television, which has an important place in mass communication, has a significant role in distance education with its special position, the way of presentation and qualities peculiar to itself. Technological developments in the field of communication can be adapted in the field of education as it is adapted to many fields of life. Thanks to the new technologies available in this field and the advantages they provide, television can already be seen as an outdated tool. Yet as long as the opportunities it provides still keep its validity, television technology is not far from the new developments. Television in distance education fulfills the functions mentioned below:

— Supporting and enhancing teaching

— Instructing

— Explaining , clarifying

— Summarizing

— Reinforcement

— Motivation and encouragement

— Using as supplementary for the other materials

— Imposing study speed (determining rate of study)

— Presenting a reference to large masses

— Changing behavior

— Presenting unreachable facts and events.

Of these special features, perhaps the most important one is that television is a very familiar and attractive source from the point of view of buyers. It is also part of our daily life. As a result of developments in communication technologies, the price of radio and television sets are dropping and their being part of our daily life has made these tools necessary in the field of education. Information transferred through of television is different from traditional education methods with respect to the audio-visual presentation. Explanations related to the subject and examples can be presented visually, so the learner gets motivated, his/her desire for learning increases, and therefore learning and remembering become easier.

Allowing thousands of people spreaded a large and distance geographic regions to receive the same program at the synchronous time, television broadcast helps overcome the problem of inequality and imbalance among the regions by providing equality in opportunities. Television transfers the events or processes through a time process peculiar to itself. In fact a process that might require a long operation can be broadcasted with main points in a short period of time.

Television may grant positive motivation such as attracting the learner?s attention to a certain point or arousing attention with the movements of the camera?s coming close, going away, and reflecting details. Invisible or virtual objects, today, can be animated with different expression methods such as cartoon films. It enables distinguished instructors to reach a large mass of students at the same time. The most distinctive specialty of television is its ability to present information to the student which other tools cannot. This is an important opportunity for students who were unable to study at a university at in other educational institutions.

Education methods, such as lecture, demonstration, and experimentation which are present in traditional education, are accepted in a different view in distance education. By using the screen as a laboratory, it is normally possible to demonstrate experiments which are too difficult to show to the students through all its phases. Television is an effective tool in expressing abstract concepts or ideas. Abstract concepts are usually produced and conveyed with words. Besides this, in making an abstract concept concrete, the role of animation and visual experimentation is very important. The limitation here is how to combine the text, which is involving information, with moving views, animation, concrete ideas, utterance and objects like pictures.

Television in the learning process could be helpful in understanding abstract ideas directly. Television is especially useful for lessons like geography, because it enables us to see whatever possible to see. Though production is a complicated process, the cost per person is low. All these features point out the superiority of television in the presentation of information. Besides these advantages, television has some serous disadvantages too which are listed below:

— The experience of watching television has been competed against a lot of activities which a viewer can do whatever want to do at the same time.

— Each of the programs is compete against to the other programs which are broadcasted from other channels.

— The viewer can prefer shifting to other program(s) or to daily another activities instead of watching program if television program does not present any attracting or watchable subject for the viewer.

One of the important disadvantages of television that it does not provide instant feedback. It?s too hard to capture the viewers reactions about the program. For this reason, the producer does not have a chance to control if the program is not watched by the viewer. In the meantime, broadcast television isn?t interactive. So that participating of the viewers are getting low. Producer never forget these important disadvantages when producing an educational television program. Besides televised broadcasts, learners can buy videotapes of these programs if they apply to the faculty. Videotapes of lectures are sent to his/her address on demand. For such demands students pay a fixed price.

The Radio and Television Broadcasting Center which has two well-equipped television and two sound studios containing out-door shooting equipment established in 1982 at Anadolu University. It makes possible all sorts of television productions with its own digital edit units, graphic, decoration, animation, archive and planning, and videotape copying departments. The center has also computer, sound and maintenance, and repair laboratories. It employs highly distinguished and experienced producers graduated from a higher education institution or got an MA degree from one of these institutions. In the departments of the center, in-service training is carried out periodically. In addition, produced programs have been revised during observation meetings in the center and the suggestions for improving the productions are put into practice.

Producing and Broadcasting Television Programs

Producing and broadcasting television programs are highly expensive. It is an easy work for an subject expert to keep talking in front of the camera. Additionally, this way does not mean for using television ineffectively as being an educational medium always. At the beginning, every unit had its own television program. Yet, with the adoption of the view that an educational television program must use all the opportunities of television, the process of television production was, in that time, re-evaluated and different methods were accepted.

In the present process, groups of experts, formed for each project, have been reviewing the existing television programs, and deciding on the renovation of the programs that have become invalid in content or in the way of presentation. The content and the form of the program to be revised or reproduced have been determined with the cooperation of the expert group, a director and a scriptwriter. After deciding what unit or subject needs to be adapted for television, the production has been realized.

For the planning of a more reliable and effective media, and for the purpose of meeting the expectations of a changing student profile, we formed a new structure within the Open Education faculty- ?Distance Education Planning Unit? (DEPU). A group of experts in their fields in this unit has begun to act to reform television programs as well as all technologies. DEPU has considered each project separately, and in the first stage it aims at determining the all objectives the students are supposed to gain. In accordance with this decision, DEPU first settles the order of information and then decides the means of tools it will be presented. And in the next stage, the established content is transformed into teaching material (books, television programs, web page etc.)

The productions which the students have not received yet, and are still in progress, are planned to be presented to the learners in coming years. During this process, a media production director (MPD), who is also in charge of television programs, is generally responsible for media conception, planning and development. The MPD, who receives academic counseling during the production process, evaluates the produced material together with Project Coordinator and the Teaching Conception Directory, and if necessary, reproduces the materials. The studies of this group cover all the projects at the Open Education

Faculty. With this respect, it has been aimed at increasing the influence of television as well as all materials and meeting the demands of the learners in a better way.

Broadcasting of the television programs of the Open Education Faculty has been realized by means of TRT (Turkish Radio and Television Institution) under the approval of the Counsel of Ministers. Prior to each academic year, the Open Education Faculty requests broadcasting time from this institution, and the hours suitable for the demands are reserved for the Open Education Faculty broadcastings. Broadcastings are shown on TRT 4, an educational channel, everyday during 24 weeks in that academic year. Day-time broadcasting which lasts 3 hours during weekday is re-broadcasted at nights. There is no repetition of the weekend broadcast on television.

Videotapes prepared according to broadcasting time are sent to TRT, Ankara. In the serials, besides the lecture programs, there are also programs such as News from Anadolu University and short programs. The Open Education Faculty television broadcasting covers a 3-hour broadcast reserved by another institution. During this time, there may be broadcasting of several lectures of the same department one after the other. Not to bore students and enable them to get ready for the next lecture, a new project was set up in this academic year. That is; between the lesson programs are sprinkled three minute-short programs. With these programs, which are generally documentary, it has been aimed at giving a cultural education as well. For this broadcasting year, nearly 70 short programs have been prepared.

Ways of using Television at Open education Faculty

Pettit, in his article titled *Learning To Swim Alone* which is about the learner support systems, points out that all distance education course elements can give learner support. According to his view, it is natural to use television, a multifunctional tool, in providing student support. Gibson emphasizes that giving support service to the students, though expensive, is a significant factor in passing from information to learning. Rowntree remarks that learners face some difficulty and problems in their own environment while they are learning and he also states that they may feel worried because of this. He lists these problems as feeling of being unable to learn on his own, fear of failure, and feeling like an outsider due to being outside of the faculty atmosphere. In short, while experts emphasize the importance of learner support, they also give emphasis to the need of individual support. With this respect, television at Open Education Faculty has a characteristics of a massive support system rather than individual one. It can be said that television at the Open Education Faculty is in a supplementary position for basic support services as well as for the content.

Television programs at the Open Education Faculty give the following services for the purpose of learner support:

— *Introductory Course Units*: Purpose of these introductory units are to introduce aim of a new course, using television in their learning period and show students the way of the study which are broadcasted at the beginning of each project.

— *Selected Units*: These program series are prepared with the purpose of supporting sections which are selected from the course syllabus. The choice of the subject matter of such programs series has been selected by the person in charge of the project, the director and the expert group. As the result of the choice of this committee, unit sections or contents within that unit section needed to be adapted for television are selected. For this reason, the number of each television program is different.

— *Full Units*: This is a concept of televising the content of unit should be a parallel with to the books. Using television at the Open Education faculty, programs have been produced in accordance with the number of units for each lesson of each project for years. While efforts for renovation continues, some program series, which are still current and produced with this consideration, have still been broadcasted. But it is also planned that these programs should be renovated in time.

Supporting Role of Television Programs

In teaching, television can be used interactively or one-way. In one-way teaching, by producing the programs beforehand, they can be delivered as videotapes or television broadcast. Contrary to this, interactive television strengthens the effect of teaching by allowing the participation of the audience. Live broadcast is a good way of broadcasting from the point of gaining interaction. Keeping this in mind, the Open Education Faculty has started two new practices in the academic year of 1998-1999.

First, from the results of mid-term and final exams processed by the Information Process Center, 10 lessons that learners have had difficulty with, were chosen. At the first stage, questions answered incorrectly for the chosen lessons were selected, and television programs, where these questions are replied by the experts, have been prepared and broadcasted. The second practice is live broadcast. In this practice, lessons decided by the Information Process Center were announced to the students before broadcasting and informed that questions could be given either by fax or telephone before or during the broadcast. Learner participation for the two-hour programs lasted five days during the weekdays was huge. The same practice was carried out for a total of 10 lessons in March and September for the academic year of 1999-2000. Live broadcasts will continue for the same period and the number before final and make-up exams in the Open Education Faculty in the future.

Supporting Identity

The aim of the ten-minute program, known as *News From Anadolu University* which added into the television programs since 1998, is to inform students and provide in them with a feeling of belonging to this faculty. The program, which is broadcasted once every two weeks for this purpose, is repeated throughout the two weeks. The content in this program is fixed during their usual meeting agenda by the news group preparing the program. The parts within the programs are as follow:

News: Besides the information directly involving students such as the academic information of the Open Education Faculty, developments, changes (in exam days, announcement of live broadcast etc.), culture-art and scientific activities scheduled at the university are also announced.

How to study?: In this part broadcasted in the academic year of 1998-1999, there was information about how the Open Education Faculty student should make use of their own educational materials as well as the important remarks for the exams.

A Portrait: In this part of the program where an Open Education Faculty student or a student graduated from the faculty was introduced, individuals who have made use of this graduation in their work life, people who chose distance education as a second study (doctors, engineer, etc.) or those who have an interesting personality or students graduated with degrees are chosen. In other word, suggestions which are encouraging and motivating the other students are reported by the student himself.

Communication Line: In this section, frequently asked questions which come from students are answered by OEF administrators..

It has been observed that this program has reached its goals. For instance, after the announcement of the test exam on the Open Education Faculty web page, the number of the visitors to this web page increased and more questions about this exam were received.

Instructional Television (ITV)

At the time of its creation more than 50 years ago, instructional television (ITV) was regarded as a means of increasing the quality of teaching by replacing the traditional classroom teacher. This vision has turned out to be a false one; today, teachers remain at the heart of the educational system. But ITV still has a role in modern education. Internet technology is bringing about a refinement of ITV's role not to supplant the teacher, but to enhance the learning the teacher provides.

Evolution of ITV

Over the following decades, an informal national

distribution system for classroom television developed, involving public broadcasting stations, school-based cable systems, educational media centers, and teachers. Today, this network includes 190 licensed PBS stations as well as cable and network stations. Most ITV programming airs on such stations in the middle of the night, sometimes featuring a whole series at once. The programs are recorded to videotape by media specialists and librarians in the school districts served, and then made available throughout the school year to teachers. In this way, hundreds of millions of students have had access to ITV programming.

The rapid advance of educational technology, the growth of the Internet, and the impending arrival of digital video transmission have all created new channels for ITV delivery. While there is no doubt that instructional video resources will continue to be used to enrich teaching, the route that these resources follow to reach students may change dramatically.

Types of ITV

Over the years, several types of ITV have developed, each of which has been helpful. Before discussing the most recent developments, it is worthwhile to review the broad categories of ITV.

Distance Learning

This school of ITV is a direct descendant of the MPATI project. Video or real-time TV is used to conduct "live" instruction. Local classroom teachers are largely uninvolved in teaching, apart from ensuring student attendance and discussing content afterwards. Recent developments such as videoconferencing, e-mail, and chat-room messaging have introduced two-way response, improving the level of interaction between the long distance teacher and the student. As a result, some successful applications of distance learning have evolved for specialist training, commercial settings, and students in remote locations. In the classroom, though, this form of ITV has limited application. No matter how engaging the content, such programs routinely fail to hold students' interest. Most schools use distance learning in moderation, limiting its use to unique events or highly specific subject areas.

Classroom Use of Broadcast Programming

The second form of ITV uses existing television programs in classroom instruction. The Nova series and Ken Burns's Civil War series are examples of programs produced originally for home viewing that have been successfully used in the classroom. This kind of programming began to appear during the 1980s due to the proliferation of the VCR, which let teachers choose when to watch programs, which programs to watch, and which segments to showcase. Though this increased the usefulness of ITV, existing programming did not always translate well for an educational setting because this mode of ITV often failed to hold classroom attention for long periods of time. What's more, if teachers decide to show small portions of a series, they must find the appropriate segment among hours of tape.

Programming Designed for the Classroom

Since the advent of the VCR, more and more programs have been produced specifically for the classroom. Whereas earlier examples of distance learning attempted to provide a video version of a traditional-style lesson, this newer type usually supplements classroom teaching. In addition, programs created specifically for classroom use can focus on specific curriculum topics.

One of the initial drawbacks of classroom-specific programming was a fixation on shows of 30 to 60 minutes in length, mimicking the format of consumer television. This mold was finally broken in the early 1990s by groundbreaking series such as "Freestyle," which sought to expand career awareness, and "Futures with Jaime Escalante," which targeted students in grades seven through twelve. As a result of extensive pre-production research, the 24-part "Futures" series was composed of 15-minute episodes. This shorter format enabled teachers to use "Futures" to establish a context for instruction and motivate student interest at the beginning of a lesson period while still allowing time to cover a curriculum topic.

Filmed and edited to broadcast standards, "Futures" sparked a re-definition of the pace and visual style of ITV programming. It rapidly became the most widely used instructional programming distributed by PBS. According to a study by Research Communications Ltd., students who watched "Futures" had a much more positive attitude toward learning math than those who did not see the program. It is this move toward shorter, more tailored programming that has made it possible to define more closely the true role of video in the classroom.

Role of Classroom Video

TV is an excellent medium for illustrating applications, describing context, and generating interest. Since it is not a truly interactive medium, though, it can neither be used to pinpoint what a student fails to understand nor remedy such misunderstandings. Here, the classroom teacher has proven to be irreplaceable. An especially effective use of video is to engage student interest by introducing a concept that is then covered in detail during class. After the video introduction, which generally lasts from 5 to 15 minutes, the teacher has enough time to discuss the topic introduced and work with students individually to ensure comprehension.

A study of classroom use of another popular program found that television, when combined with other activities, could both alter entrenched attitudes towards math and improve student performance. The research focused on the Peabody Award-winning series The Eddie Files, which is produced for elementary-school students. Each episode focuses on a topic from the elementary curriculum such as fractions, estimation, or statistics. In pre-test interviews, 90% of the students interviewed found math "boring." After watching episodes over a two-month period and completing lessons from the series' teacher guide, 75% of those students no longer found math boring. The number of students who wanted a career that required math increased by 14% in the second poll. This later poll also found that students were better able to define concepts covered in the TV series, more likely to give correct answers to questions, and better able to list applications of the curriculum topics that had been addressed.

A study conducted by Chen and Hodder, focusing primarily on career education programming, helped underscore the elements of effective classroom television. The authors examined a ten-year track of formative and summative research conducted by the Foundation for Advancements in Science and Education (FASE), which created Futures and The Eddie Files, as well as other highly-regarded ITV programs. They concluded that shorter programming was of higher value and greater impact and that video proved most useful when used to support, rather than replace, the teacher.

Out of the video boom of the 1980s came another important ITV development: the production of teachers' guides and other materials to supplement programming. Some producers have found that well-produced guidebooks can increase classroom use of video by a factor of five to ten. The arrival of the Internet promised to alleviate some of these concerns. The Web provided publishers with a convenient repository for updated guidebooks. Yet while 99% of teachers report that they have ready access to the Internet or computers, only 39% say that they actually use such technology frequently to create instructional materials. Having an Internet connection, then, is not enough. As many teachers find when they look online for help with lesson plans, the user is typically bombarded by thousands of hits on any given subject. The wealth of data must be made more focused and easier to use.

Internet and ITV

Whatever current practices may be, there is no doubt that teachers' use of the Internet to find and create lesson materials will increase dramatically in the future. It is through the Internet that video offers its greatest promise for educators. In an effort to capitalize on the advantages of video while conserving classroom time, many teachers show two or three minute segments from longer programs. Responding to this practice and to the demand for teachers to address specific national and state guidelines, ITV is creating a new "micro-documentary" format. Shorter clips can heighten video's usefulness by precisely underscoring a curriculum point. However, no formula exists for reconciling what producers could shoot and what teachers might need on a given day. The most feasible solution is to make a wide range of materials available in an easily navigable catalogue that allows individual teachers to choose what they need.

Recognizing that a vast archive would be necessary to meet the needs of teachers, the channel began by acquiring exclusive rights to more than 1,000 hours of award-winning footage shot by FASE productions. This base is being expanded through partnership agreements with Adventure Pictures (for environmental and geographic sciences), the Mount Wilson Institute, and other companies and institutes. The Futures Channel has already produced several hundred short clips that highlight real-world applications of educational concepts. These clips form the core of a database that allows teachers to search quickly for resources-videos, lesson materials, and student activities-on specific concepts in math, science, technology, and the arts.

According to a Cahners In-stat Group study, 45 million homes will be using broadband by 2002. Within three to six years, most schools will have Internet connections that permit video downloading. In the interim, alternative methods of distribution will have to be used. One possibility is for teachers to view clips in a low bandwidth format that works adequately on a 56k modem, decide what they want, and either upload the material via CD-ROM or access it over a school or district network.

In the near future, then, teachers will have access to support materials and vast libraries of educational video content, from seconds to hours in length. These will be indexed in such a way that the teacher can rapidly find relevant clips, view excerpts, and find links to related lesson activities. This material will be catalogued according to grade level, subject, and various local, state, and national standards.

Instructional television is finally finding its niche. While teachers will continue to play the pivotal role in education, ITV will play a supporting role, catching student interest, focusing attention on specific subjects, and emphasizing key points. The further evolution of ITV must be guided by the necessity to harness new resources in the manner that best helps classroom teachers.

Teleconferencing

Moore and Kearsley define teleconferencing in terms of describing "the interaction of students and instructors via some form of telecommunications technology. There are four different types of teleconferencing.: audio, audiographics, video, and computer." Teleconferencing is provided using a variety of communication technologies such as satellite, microwave, and Instructional Television Fixed Service(ITFS). Services include producing, hosting, or broadcasting satellite downlinks, uplinks, or 2-way teleconferences to a number of locations. The studio classrooms have 3-camera production capability, an audio distribution system connecting remote locations and the studio on campus, and A-V equipment such as slide projectors, an overhead graphics camera and pad suitable for showing visual aids, 3/4" or SVHS videotape recorders, computers etc.

Computers can interface with the TV system for showing graphics or other visual aids and the Internet. Audioconferencing is most common and least expensive form of teleconferencing. Audiographic teleconferencing systems involve the use of computer or facsimile technology to transmit visuals to support the audio. Some computer systems allow the transmission of graphics, programs, and data, where each site sees anything on the instructor computer screen, besides hearing the audio. Audigraphic systems are good for classes that involve a lot of illustration, such as equations, or computer applications. Videoconferencing can be transmitted via satellite, cable, or standard telephone lines. It requires compressing the videos and several equipment.

Videoconferencing allows learners and instructors to interact face-to-face. The site below is a site for a class that is being taught by videoconferencing. The site answers questions about videoconferencing technology, why, when, and how to use it. Using high-quality compressed video and audio technology, this videoconference/distance education classroom is networked with all the University of California and California State campuses. This videoconference/ distance education classroom is also capable of connecting with other sites across the state, the nation and the world.

Computer Conferencing allows students and instructors to interact via a computer network. This interaction can be through e-mail messages, file transfer, chat rooms, real audio and video, and others. With the fast progress in computer technology, computer conferencing is taking its place in educational technology. Computer conferencing provides good quality, easy to use, and cost-efficient way of interaction.

Computer-Based Instruction

Computer-Based Instruction (CBI) refers to instructional programs that the student uses alone on a personal computer. The program is usually provided on CD-ROM, in multimedia format (graphics, text, sound, and video). Even though CD-ROM-based instruction provides effective presentations and cost-effective medium, it is not commonly used in distance education programs, since it does not provide dynamic content and needed interaction between the learner and the instructor. The site below has a slide show about using computer technology in distance education. It divides computer-based instruction into Multimedia-based (like CD-ROM) and Internet-based (like email and WWW).

Web-based Instruction in Education

With the fast growth of the Internet, and the fast progress of communication, the world wide web is a new promising medium for distance learning. With the enormous number of resources available online, and the increasing number of people who have access to the Internet, web-based instruction is considered one of the fastest media for teaching and learning. The world wide web provides a cost-effective, technology rich, and interactive medium.

Because a myriad of computers and programs are part of the Internet, incompatibility problems can result because information is created using different computers and software. In 1989, a group of scientists at the European Laboratory for Particle Physics (CERN) in Geneva, Switzerland began developing an Internet tool that would link information produced by all of the CERN researchers. The tool provided a way to link textual information on different computers and created by different scientists. The object was to overcome issues of incompatibility and utilize a new way of linking made possible by computers, called "hypertext". Rather than presenting information in a linear or hierarchical fashion, hypertext permits information to be linked in a web-like structure. Nodes of information can be linked to other nodes of information in multiple ways. As a result, users can dynamically criss-cross the information web using pieces in the order most convenient to them.

The World-Wide Web (WWW) provides users with a uniform and convenient means of accessing the vast resources of the Internet. In 1993, the National Center for Supercomputing Applications (NCSA) at the University of Illinois pushed the CERN scientists' idea further by creating a software tool called Mosaic. Mosaic is an easy to use graphical user interface that permits text, graphics, sound and video to be hyperlinked. Mosaic was the first of the Internet tools that are now referred to as " Web browsers". Other well-known browsers include Netscape (the first commercial browser developed by some of the programmers involved with the Mosaic project) and Microsoft's Internet Explorer.

Web browsers permit users to connect to the Internet and facilitate accessing information located on another remote computer. The Web browser links to the remote computer just long enough so that the information you need can be sent to your computer for you to view. Documents created to be viewed by a browser are formatted using Hypertext Markup Language (HTML).

HTML solves incompatibility problems by using standardized tags which indicate such things as whether a piece of text should be plain, bold, italic, or linked to another piece of text. Pages of information on a computer formatted with HTML and accessible to someone with a Web browser, are referred to as "home pages" or "Web pages".

The WWW and Web browsers have made the Internet a more user-friendly environment. The ability to integrate graphics, text, and sound into a single tool means that novice users do not have to struggle with such a steep learning curve. In addition, organizations and individuals can create home pages independently and link to other home pages on their own computers or to pages created by others on different computer systems.

For educators, the WWW provides an exciting new opportunity for distance teaching and learning. The WWW can be used by the distance educator to build a classroom home page. The home page can cover information about the class including the syllabus, exercises, literature references, and instructor's biography. The instructor can also provide links to information on the WWW that would be useful to students in the class (e.g., research data on agricultural markets, global climate change, or space missions). Other links can access library catalogs or each student's individual home page. In addition, the home page can link students to a discussion list or listserv that set up for student communication. It is also a relatively simple matter to use the homepage to create forms that students can fill out and that will end up being sent to you as an e-mail message.

Distance educators who are ready to develop a web presence, should avoid the following pitfalls:

— *Rushing in without a master plan*. Don't get so caught up in learning HTML and developing the home page that the purpose for developing your presence on the WWW is lost. Spend less time struggling with HTML, developing amusing graphics or playing with possible background and more time considering the purpose and content of the home page. Before you start your home page:

— *Think about your reason for developing a Web presence*. Will your home page be a stand alone course or will you be using it in conjunction with other technologies such as video or audio? Sound instructional design principles apply to home pages just as with any other materials prepared for a course.

— *Become familiar with new software tools for developing home pages*. Computer software tools such as HotMetal and

HotDog mean that anyone familiar with using word processing software can develop a good looking and functional home page. Reviews of other such computer software tools are available on the WWW and many of them can be downloaded for a free trial.

— *Utilize information that already has been developed for your course.* If you already have your notes and syllabi in word processed form, make use of tools such as HotDog to format them for distribution on the WWW.

— *Look at what is already available.* Hundreds of home pages have already been developed for courses. Some of these home pages allow students to complete an entire course from the WWW and others are developed in conjunction with lectures delivered on-campus or by video or audio.

— *Laying out home pages poorly and inconsistently.* To avoid ugly and confusing home pages, consider the following:

— Consulting sites on the WWW which provide information on home page layout and style. A popular site is the Web Style Manual.

— Utilizing a consistent format for each of your pages. Based on suggestions made by the above mentioned style manuals, develop a consistent format for each web page. While colored or patterned backgrounds can be used on homepages, plain grey or white backgrounds make text easier to read.

— *Keeping page lengths short.* Your main index should jump to a lot of shorter pages. In cases where page information is long, index internally so that the student can jump to specific information as needed.

— Maximizing links to internal information and minimizing links to external information. The purpose of your home page is to provide information on a specific subject area. Only provide external links to home pages that provide useful related information for your students.

— Using unnecessarily large graphics or including sound/video clips. Consider that while graphics can add appeal to a home page, a large number of Internet users are still accessing the Internet using a 14.4K modem. Graphic images which are 20K to 40K are acceptable for people with 14.4K modems. Pages which take too long to download frustrate students and may force them to beat a hasty retreat. If your home page requires extensive use of graphics to demonstrate points, warn your students. If you plan to use sound or video clips, you will need to be sure that all of your distant students have access to computers that have sound and video cards installed in them.

— Letting the home page become out-of-date. The home page should be an ongoing part of course development. Make sure that you add or change information as necessary. Periodically verify whether other home pages to which you are linking still exist.

The home page should help your students to find necessary course information, learn the material, and get involved in thinking about the course material. Properly designed home pages will encourage thought, discussion and active participation by your distant students. The following elements can be included in your class home page:

— *Course & Instructor Information* - Include such items as course topics to be covered, your office hours, textbook information, course objectives, and grading policies.

— *Class Communication* - Provide access to your e-mail, link to discussion groups that you have set up for student-to-student communication, and create forms that your students can use to report problems or provide biographical information about themselves.

— *Assignments and Tests* - Distribute assignments and tests, provide for online completion or submission, and give solutions, hints, or samples of what you expect.

— *Material covered in the classroom* - Make lecture notes and handouts available either as web pages or as downloadable files.

— *Demonstrations, Animation, Video, Audio* - This is more complex than other suggestions and will require that your students have access to computers with sound and video cards.

— *Reference Material* - List materials in print and electronic form that supplement the textbook. To avoid copyright problems, electronic articles should either be written by you or in the public domain (e.g., government documents or are already available on the WWW with author's permission to distribute). In addition, provide links to other pages which cover information on the topic, similar courses that may also be available on WWW, your university library, and other on-campus resources that may help your student complete the course.

10

Communication and Sustainable Development

Communication has become a key feature of sustainable development. Indeed, "communication for development" has become a recognized field among many development decision-makers. The opening for the communication field comes from the recognition that in sustainable development there are multiple stakeholders all generating and exchanging information. There is, therefore, a need for building bridges, linking different viewpoints and creating a common "language" among different stakeholders. The contrasting interpretations of reality between rural folk and policy makers, or between scientists and field staff, are the challenges faced by the field of communication for development. These are the entry points for strategically designed communication efforts aimed at linking different stakeholders.

Communication for development is about aiding different types of actors interested in understanding needs and assessing opportunities jointly; it is about providing them with the methods and media to reach common meaning, and about enabling them to negotiate with other actors with contrasting perceptions and interests.

The need for sustainable development is generally accepted as a desirable goal and that multiple stakeholders are involved in providing and using information towards this goal. "In sustainable development, everyone is a user and provider of infor-mation considered in the broad sense. That includes data, information, appropriately packaged experience and knowledge. The need for information arises at all levels, from that of senior decision makers at the national and international levels to the grass-roots and individual levels".

The recognition that there are multiple relevant stakeholders, all of whom use and provide information, constitutes an entry point for the field of communication for development. Communication refers to the two-way exchange of information, a feature which is a key component to effective development. As is argued in a recent discussion paper on information technology: "There is substantial evidence that without two-way information flows development efforts fail".

The fundamental role of communication is a significant step ahead in the context of sustainable development. In many sectors information has been understood as a public relations exercise aimed at raising public awareness, or merely as a mechanism to transfer knowledge and technology in a uni-directional mode. Today there is growing recognition that the impact of such approaches is limited or short-lived and additional efforts are needed to give voice to the knowledge and perspectives of people at the grassroots since they are no longer willing to be treated passive recipients of information.

For the last two decades, communication for development practitioners have acted as brokers between the needs of rural people, different kinds of development interventions, and quickly evolving communication and information technologies. This is a field of development which evolves at a particularly rapid pace as communication practitioners seek to reconcile technological innovation with rural peoples' needs and constraints.

Brokering between the technology and the needs of rural people is one key concern of development communication practitioners. Questions always arise about accessibility to media in remote areas, about how to reconcile costs, and about the appropriateness of different media for different purposes. When the first steps were taken by the Food and Agriculture Organization of the United Nations (FAO) in the mid 1970s in Peru to use video as a tool to "recover, preserve and reproduce peasant knowledge", the organization was critiqued because of the seemingly inappropriate use of what appeared to be too sophisticated a medium for a rural setting. "Much of FAO's historical success with communication for development approaches has involved the use of a medium that many development planners first dismissed as too 'high-tech' and as being 'inappropriate technology' when used by agencies working with rural and agricultural communities". As it turned out, the FAO project in Peru paved the way for what is today common practice in many rural development projects: the use of video as a cost-effective tool to support group training.

Twenty years later, the field of communication for development faces an equivalent challenge with regard to the use of the Internet in rural development. What role will the Internet play in rural development? Who will benefit? Which sectors need to come together to provide the telecommunication infrastructure? Is there adequate software and hardware available in each country? What types of training, planning, and financing is required? Is it a development tool as such? Can it serve to mediate policy dialogue and enhance decision-making at local level? A recent report sets the course for this challenge and summarises the common elements of successful rural and agricultural Internet and communication and information systems .

Technological innovation in the information media is not the only reason for the hasty speed at which communication for development evolves. Another reason is the evolving understanding of development and the emergence of new approaches and paradigms. The WCED document introduced the notion of sustainable development. The notion of sustainability has led to new insight into the challenges of development where the process of building alliances and seeking common agendas among stakeholders with different interests becomes as important as the output itself.

A focus on learning means a focus on people as the protagonists of development. UNDP's report focused attention on the human dimension of development, thus opening the door for participatory approaches that engage rural people in assessing needs, planning and implementing development interventions. The above key documents have expanded the realm of activities where communication for development can play an enabling role by bringing attention to previously disregarded human and environmental issues rises to the challenge with practical examples of communication as applied to a range of contexts, from its use at the grassroots to enhance the exchange of ideas, all the way to the policy level.

A clarifying perspective by proposing three different roles which communication for development can play in natural resource management:

— explaining biophysical information (increasingly with the aim of creating new perspectives rather than transferring pre-packaged solutions);

— enacting and promoting policies, (increasingly there is a trend towards interactive policy making rather moving away form persuasive advertising approaches);

— giving a voice to different stakeholders to engage in platforms where negotiation among different parties can take place with regard to natural resources.

The third role constitutes the less explored and more promising dimension of communication in the context of sustainable development. Linear transmission of information is no longer the only focus; rather, the orchestration of platforms of negotiation among multiple actors is most important. When speaking about platforms, communication clearly becomes a facilitating force for stakeholder negotiations; if we consider the three roles, communication provides a meeting ground for information exchange, public awareness, and stakeholder negotiation.

Communication for development is now a field closely associated with the very process of development planning, decision-making, implementation and evaluation. Communication is no longer marginal to the process as a public relations effort. The sustainable agriculture is only possible when resource conservation technologies are available, along with local institutions and organizations who in turn are supported by enabling external institutions. These three conditions, however, can only thrive under the umbrella of a supportive policy environment. If we are to focus our attention on the three basic conditions - adequate technologies, local organization, and enabling external institutions - then what is the role of communication for development? In this paper it is argued that communication is an enabling process behind each of the above conditions. Adequate technology can only be developed with the participation of all relevant stakeholders, and this, among other factors, requires a common "language" among them for the exchange of perspectives to participate in technology development . Local organizations and groups capable of acting on sustainable resource management plans require new skills and knowledge that communication for development can enhance. Moreover, they also require a voice to highlight their judgement on priorities and implementation so as to negotiate on equal footing with outsider institutions. Enabling external institutions need to establish a rapport with the local groups to enable a trustful, learning relationship to emerge. Each of these activities requires some form of communication support.

The facilitators of this interaction require the skill and professionalism to articulate this relationship using a range of communication media . According to FAO, the types of capacities these new professionals are expected to have include:

— a capacity to dialogue and cooperate among sectors, institutions and different interest groups;

— a capacity to promote sustained participation by rural communities;

— an ability to collect, analyse and use information for different purposes;

— a capacity to identify, prepare and negotiate projects;

— a knowledge of relevant research and technology.

These capacities are very different from those which conventional professionals in development receive during their training. Indeed, the capacities proposed resemble those which NGOs aim to develop within the communities they assist. The following list from the NGO World Neighbours is relevant:

— capacity to identify, develop and extend improved technologies and practices;

— capacity to mobilize local (human and financial) resources: to recruit and motivate farmer experimenters and agricultural promoters, and to generate revenue to cover core operating expenses;

— capacity to negotiate with external agencies (e.g., research and extension services, credit institutions, donors);

— capacity for inter-village collaboration: coordination of villages in the same area and communication with farmer organizations in other areas for mutual learning;

— capacity for programme management: diagnosing problems, assessing needs, planning, setting objectives, budgeting, monitoring and evaluation, reporting;

— capacity to organize itself (i.e. have appropriate structures) for implementing self-development activities, such as identifying, testing and evaluating new technologies, and farmer-to-farmer extension;

— capacity for broad-based leadership with a mobilizing vision, initiative and ability to conceptualize and raise awareness;

— capacity for democratic, transparent and representative decision-making, which takes the needs of different socio-economic groups and genders into account.

In fact, we need a new communication professional who is comfortable with the interface between the natural resource disciplines, multiple stakeholders and the management of conflicts among them. In addition to the new professionals, the development of appropriate technologies requires input from a number of actors. Ideally, the list should include rural folk, field staff of extension organizations, NGOs, research institutes and, increasingly important in many countries, local municipal authorities. This is especially the case when referring to the management of natural resources and when we are talking about watershed management, rather than single households or farms. Experience has shown that top-down transfer of technologies has proven inadequate for resource-poor areas where rural people face complex environments with site-specific conditions which require site-specific attention. While the transfer of technology model has proven ineffective for these areas, new perspectives and approaches that take heed of the multiple actors with stakes in the use and sustainability of the environment are emerging . The approach seeks to identify the social actors involved in natural resource management with the aim of grasping their relationships, analysing them, and coming to agreements on how to modify and improve the networking among the actors. Understanding existing patterns of information exchange is an effective entry point for planning communication activities . The focus, beyond planning, is towards establishing conditions for learning to take place among the interested parties as learning communities or platforms.

Communication for development can be an enabling tool for local organizations and groups to gain the confidence, skill and knowledge to become protagonists in sustainable development. As various experiences have demonstrated, a starting point is the use of communication media to help local groups identify problems, document them using traditional or electronic media, and communicate them to local and national authorities. Skill and knowledge exchange at the level of problem identification are crucial to the task of agreeing on plans to overcome problems. There is a growing body of experience in the use of visual media to assist rural, often illiterate groups, to participate in action research and engage in platforms for negotiation. The growing number of organizations with relevant experience in the use of visuals to enhance local groups' voice in development activities - from appraisal, action-research, and evaluation - across different disciplines is impressive In this context, the work of the London-based International Institute for Environment and Development (IIED) and of the Institute for Development Studies merit attention with regard to their experience in developing participatory appraisal tools. IIED and IDS are pioneers in the development of participatory rural appraisal (PRA) tools using simple graphics to give rural people a voice. A great deal of relevant literature on practical methods under the overall title of "participatory learning and action" is available from both organizations.

Efforts are underway to explore participatory development communication. One such research programme in West Africa focuses attention to "... horizontal approaches that involve encouraging dialogue centred on problem analysis and a search for solutions, as well as bottom-up approaches that aim to raise the awareness of decision-makers. These approaches are based on a process of community communication. In terms of its overall thrust, the programme takes an interactive and participatory approach that stresses the interrelationships that exist in practice among the main line of action.

Policy Dimensions

In the past communication was interpreted as a public relations exercise, or as merely a transfer of technology tool. While communication for development remains an important information delivery tool, it is the *information* aspect which tends to dominate the role assigned to communication, especially in governmental organizations. The role of the Internet may once again reinforce this aspect, unless a true demand-capacity from the grassroots is able to match and select relevant information. On the other hand, the other three dimensions tend to be taken up by other sectors and increasingly by non-governmental organizations.

It remains a challenge to institutionalize these dimensions of communication; as Pretty rightly points out, an enabling policy environment is required. Not only that, but in the case of development communication, the dimensions tend to bypass traditional ministry boundaries. Indeed, the Communication for Development Group at FAO has succeeded in orchestrating the development of National Development Communication Strategies. These efforts are built on the recognition that development communication is a partner to any discipline where information and perspectives need to be exchanged among different stakeholders. These national strategies enable governments to channel resources to communication activities and investments in a coherent manner recognising that communication provides a support to a number of areas including forestry, agriculture, natural resources, health, water and sanitation, nutrition, to name a few. FAO has had ample experience in all continents in trying to institutionalize develop-ment communication units in governments. The success, at best, has been partial and new inter-institutional arrangements with NGOs and possibly the private sector are needed to ensure that all aspects of development communication remain financially viable and at the service of rural development . The notion of sustainability has led to a better understanding of communication as a development field and to a recognition of its multiple dimensions. A common feature of agricultural extension organizations, however, is the use of communication only for message production and public awareness raising. Public sector organizations have managed to use communication to facilitate participation and stakeholder platforms. Even where investments have been made in communication to support extension, the tendency has been to focus attention on the media hardware at the expense of the content, software or capacity building. Relatively little attention has been dedicated to the relevance of the message to different audiences' predicaments, and more effort has been put into the equipment needed to broadcast the message. The poor track record of top-down information campaigns, it is surprising that coercive approaches are still advocated in isolation from the other conditions which enable rural population to participate in their own development.

Shifting paradigms

There is encouraging evidence of a new paradigm in natural resource management which starts with a people-first approach and places great attention on participatory, decentralized planning. Worldwide, participatory approaches in watershed conservation projects are being tested, often with the sobering realization that such efforts need to also include coherent capacity-building, institutional support and conducive policies. A more systematic analysis of the roles and impact of different actors in natural resource management is leading the way to a better understanding of who needs to be consulted in developing alternative management strategies.

Communication for development can become a powerful tool, a meeting ground, for sustainable development when attention is given to:

— a supportive policy environment

— capable human resources within local organizations

— a flexible, coordinated external institutional context

— a strategic use of communication and information activities designed to meet specific needs and applications with a balanced approach to the three roles of communication: transfer of ideas, insight and technology; awareness raising on policy and institutional issues; and facilitating communication among actors with a stake in natural resource management.

Third World approach

There is much controversy around the use of videotape recording technology in community work. One reason is that video is often incorrectly used by people who see its enormous potential for community work but do not have access to the kind of experience and knowledge that will help them to make the right decisions about obtaining video equipment for field work or about using correctly the video equipment they have already.

Many countries have suffered in their first contacts with video as a tool in learning for the following reasons, among others:

- those seeking to introduce the technology are not aware of what is required to make it and keep it an effective tool for learning, nor do they know where to go to seek sound advice;
- the teachers and trainers are sometimes outsiders with lack of knowledge of local conditions and customs that will affect production/distribution/maintenance. When their projects fail, they often blame the technology, not their own deficiencies;
- international agencies are not as well equipped as they should be to give sound advice;
- foreign governments are often well-intentioned in supplying video equipment but their donations are often ill-conceived and made without any real understanding of what is required to make the technology and effective tool in community work, nor do they know enough about its strengths and limitations;
- equipment manufacturers' technical training is from the perspective of the salesman. They do not usually offer truly critical assessments of their products, nor are they aware of field conditions under which video equipment is often used in community work.

Empowering Communities in the Information Society

There are many intellectuals and policy makers, most of whom have access to modern information and communication technology, who question whether people, particularly ordinary, mostly poor people in developing countries, really need these technologies and warn us about its potential harmful effects. Many of them feel that drilling wells for clean water, building roads, provision of primary health care and schools for teaching people to read and write are much more important for improving poor peoples health and living conditions in general than providing them with computers and access to data networks. The information available through networks, they argue, is chiefly produced in the west and for the west and computer mediated discussion groups spread western values and culture and threaten the survival of local culture. Moreover, opponents to free access to information note that cyberspace is full of "garbage" and "pollutes" innocent people and children with western perversions. Some people feel that potentially dangerous extremist groups and subversive terrorists can use the networks to spread their distorted messages and influence the ignorant masses. And then, there are the problems of data security and copyright.Roads are of course important but, say those who believe in the potential benefits of the "information society" for poor people in the developing world, so are telecommunications. Access to telephones and faxes, they argue, reduces the need for people to travel and their feeling of being isolated and improves the efficiency of transport of goods. Thus, these telecommunications tools reduce transportation costs, improve availability of essential goods and contribute to improving living conditions and to reducing pollution. They may also contribute to saving lives in case of man-made or natural disasters and reduce the harmful consequences of such disasters. In difficult terrain it may take years to build roads and still many rural communities can only be reached by foot and horses and donkeys are the principal means of transport. In contrast, modern terrestrial and satellite radio-communication systems can be provided in a relatively short time, also in very remote and isolated areas and reduce drastically the need for cumbersome travelling.

Nobody questions the vital importance of schools and primary health care centres in rural and isolated communities. However, it is difficult to attract qualified teachers and doctors to work in such areas when there are no means of keeping in touch with colleagues and friends and with developments in their fields. The promoters of the information society claim that the quality of public services, including health, education and security could be immensely improved by means of modern information and telecommunication technologies. Access to the rapidly increasing, electronically stored information and knowledge resources in the field of health and education, including courses in basic hygiene, literacy, water management and environment protection as well as in occupational fields of relevance to rural communities such as agriculture, animal husbandry, handicrafts, business administration, etc., and the possibility to call the specialist doctor when needed, are as important for the well being of the people as drilling wells and providing primary health centres. Access to such facilities would also contribute to retaining qualified professionals and attract more of them to work in rural and remote areas, i.e. reduce the migration to urban centres or even reverse this trend.

Those in favour also argue that access to information and communication technologies is vital for economic development and for any enterprise to compete in today's global economy, and that generation of economic wealth and a more equal distribution of this wealth, within countries and globally, is a condition sine qua non for the poor to improve their living conditions, and thus also for social and cultural development.

As regards the "cyberspace garbage", they would claim that the advantages of being able to timely access relevant information and "knowledge networks" and having the possibility and right to freely communicate ones own opinions and values to the rest of the world, by far outweighs the potential dangers of providing access to this global forum. Some people even consider the right to communicate as a fundamental condition for the development of democracy and for global peaceful coexistence.

Clearly, the development of the infrastructure and of people's awareness of the possibilities offered by modern information and communication technologies and their capabilities to make use of such technologies will not happen unless their is a political will and the right policies are in place.

Access to networks

To adopt the adequate policies is a necessary but not sufficient conditions for bringing people into the information society. Timely access to information and knowledge requires also an adequate, widespread telecommunication infrastructure and in this respect the global picture is still rather gloomy. Moreover, the telecommunication infrastructure in developing countries is concentrated to the larger cities and in many countries virtually non-existent in rural and remote areas. As regards access to information and data networks, notably the Internet, the discrepancies between the rich and the poor and between urban and rural areas are even more accentuated. It is estimated that more than half of the world's population have never used a telephone. The gap between those who have access to these vital resources and those who have not is widening also in many rich countries. Even in advanced countries there are large pockets of socially or geographically isolated population strata, which either don't have access to adequate telecommunications, can't afford modern information and communication facilities, or just lack the required skills to use them.

Multipurpose community telecentres

The concept of "multipurpose community telecentres", a shared information and communication facility for people in rural and isolated areas was initially introduced in the Scandinavian countries some 20 years ago as means of improving access to telematics in rural and isolated areas. A community telecentre is here defined as a multipurpose centre, providing IT and telecommunication facilities, user support and training for members of a community who cannot afford such facilities on an individual basis and/or do not have the skills to use such tools. The set up and applications supported by such centres vary considerably. In its simplest form, widely introduced in developing countries, such centres may provide public telephone, and fax services only and be handled by the local shopkeeper, for example. However, such "telecentres", often called "telekiosks" are usually established in densely populated areas and hardly qualify as "multipurpose" centres.

At the other end of the scale there are telecentres with offices for local small business and "teleworkers" and equipped with computers, printer, photocopier, etc. Such centres would provide access to data networks for e-mail, file transfer, access to electronic libraries and databases, government and community information systems, market and price information, environmental watch, etc. as well as facilities and equipment for teletraining and telemedicine. Some may also provide facilities, equipment and training for local production of radio and TV broadcasting programmes. Such multipurpose centres of course also need specialised support staff for the different applications, in particular facilitators for distance learning programmes, and including staff for the management and operation of the service and for maintenance of the equipment. The viability of such centres vary. Most of them were initially established with substantial government support, which was gradually withdrawn. Some centres were then forced to close, particularly in affluent societies, where the telecommunication infrastructure is quite good, but also in rural areas. People tend to acquire the necessary IT and communication equipment once they have seen the value of these tools. In these cases the community telecentres have played an impo-tant role in the marketing of new services, which is not always recog-nised by the service providers and operators who benefit from this.

There are many similar centres, e.g., business centres in hotels, distance learning centres, telemedicine centres library information centres (located in libraries), and, more recently, "Internet cafes". However, in contrast to the community telecentres, these are essential single purpose centres and tend to be located in densely populated areas. One solution in remote areas may be to establish a "virtual telecentre" where different applications are located in different buildings, but using a common telecom infrastructure and common support.

It is important to recognise that the large majority of the 70 to 80 percent of the population in developing countries who live in rural and remote communities have little if any money to spend on such "luxuries" as information and communications. Yet some of us believe that they need information and communication facilities as much if not more than densely populated urban communities. Access to public telephones and a fax would already be a significant improvement of their living conditions, but the provision of modern information and communication technologies holds the promise of promoting social, economic and cultural development at quite a different scale. Paradoxically, there may be cases when the provision of such services are more cost-effective than the provision of basic services only.

Multipurpose community telecentres seems to offer the means to make such services widely accessible to populations in remote and isolated areas, where it is hardly conceivable to provide separate facilities and support for each application and where there is the need to maximise the number of users to make optimum use of the common, expensive telecommunication infrastructure. Deprived urban slum areas are not geographically, but socially isolated and have many characteristics in common with rural remote areas. Therefore, in such cases community telecentres may be an appropriate solution.

Bibliography

Bain, George. Gotcha! *How The Media Distort the News*. Toronto: Key Porter Books, 1994.

Ball-Rokeach, Sandra J. and Cantor, Muriel G. (Editors).*Media: Audience and Social Structure*. London: Sage, 1986.

Bartel, Diane. *Putting on Appearances: Gender and Advertising*. Temple University Press, 1988.

Barwise, Patrick and Ehrenberg, Andrew. *Television and its Audience*. London: Sage, 1989.

Blum, Eleanor. *Basic Books in The Mass Media* (Second Edition). Chicago: University of Illinois Press, 1980

Buckingham, David (Editor). *Reading Audiences: Young People and The Media*. Manchester: Manchester University Press, 1993.

Cooke, Liz (Editor). *Media Studies Bibliography*. London: BFI, 1984.

Davies, Maire Messenger. *Television is Good For Your Kids*. London: Hilary Shipman, 1989.

Dyer, Gillian. *Advertising as Communication*. London: Methuen 1982.

Elliott, Deni (Editor). *Responsible Journalism*. London: Sage, 1986.

Greenfield, Patricia Marks. *Mind and Media: The Effects of Television*. Computers and Video Games. London: Fontana, 1984.

Gunter, Barrie and McAleer, Jill L. *Children and Television: The One Eyed Monster*? London: Routledge, 1990.

Hartley, John. *Understanding News.* New York: Routledge, 1982.

Hodge, Bob and Tripp, David. *Children and Television: A Semiotic Approach.* Cambridge: Polity Press, 1986.

Jhally, Sut. *The Codes of Advertising: Fetishism and The Political Economy of Meaning in The Consumer Society.* New York: Routledge, 1990.

Leiss, William et al. *Social Communication in Advertising: Persons. Products and Images of Well-Being* (Second Edition: Revised and Enlarged). New York: Routledge 1990.

Manoff, Robert Karl and Schudson, Michael (Editors). *Readingthe News.* New York: Pantheon, 1986.

Nelson, Joyce. *Sultans of Sleeze: Public Relations and The Media.* Toronto: Between The Lines Press, 1989.

Singer, Benjamin D. *Advertising and Society.* Don Mills: Addison-Wesley, 1987.

Stephens, Mitchell. *A History of the News*: From Drum to Satellite. New York: Viking, 1988.

Index